Church Unplugged

Church Unplugged

Remodelling church without losing your soul

David Male

Authentic

MILTON KEYNES ● COLORADO SPRINGS ● HYDERABAD

14 13 12 11 10 09 08 7 6 5 4 3 2 1

First published 2008 by Authentic Media
9 Holdom Avenue, Bletchley, Milton Keynes, MK1 1QR, UK
1820 Jet Stream Drive, Colorado Springs, CO 80921, USA
OM Authentic Media
Medchal Road, Jeedimetla Village, Secunderabad 500 055, A.P.
www.authenticmedia.co.uk

Authentic Media is a division of IBS-STL U.K., limited by guarantee, with its
Registered Office at Kingstown Broadway, Carlisle, Cumbria CA3 0HA.
Registered in England & Wales No. 1216232. Registered charity 270162

British Library Cataloguing in Publication Data

A catalogue record for this book is available from the British Library

ISBN-13: 978-1-85078-792-1

Cover design by MOOSE77
Print Management by Adare
Printed in Great Britain by J.H. Haynes & Co., Sparkford

Contents

Foreword

I get energy from seeing other people do what I couldn't;
climbing sheer rock faces, taming tigers or starting fresh
kinds of churches. I met Dave first in January 1999 as he
was setting out on the adventure called the Net.
Immediately I was drawn to his energy and integrity. It has
been a privilege to be part of the steering group ever since.

So I am deeply pleased that this book has come out, for
several reasons. The most profound are strategic and
theological. I have been convinced, since the mid 1990s,
that any church, whether local or national, which bases
its identity and mission around territory is deceived. This
is not where the future lies. We need to learn how to
respond to the dominant social reality of network. We
need to stop thinking that we must identify with people
where they are and learn that incarnation is more closely
linked to identifying with people *how* they are. This book
welcomes and enters the world of network. It is crucial
we take note and learn. We need stories to make real the
change. The Net in Huddersfield represents what this
journey looks like in practice.

I also like the spread and balance of the book. Missional
priorities and lessons are balanced by the conviction that

church is firstly communal and organic. Planting church is far more creative and demanding than adding to an existing one or just copying it. Dave's book adds depth to our understanding of how this is done well.

The last reason is personal. I have known the Net since it was an egg, so it is a delight to have watched it be born, take off and fly. What some thought was an ugly duckling is showing quite a few very white feathers. Dave and I have been through the thick and thin of that complicated progression. I have watched him as friend and mentor, finding out what works, celebrating and despairing, planning and improvising. I trust telling the story will sow further seeds that can lead to more churches. They will need to find their own way; to take the principles and translate them faithfully but creatively, into further contexts. Thanks, Dave, for the ride, and now for the travel guide.

George Lings
Sheffield, November 2007

Introduction

The hardest service I have ever had to take was on Sunday 2nd April 2006. I had to stand up in front of the Net Church, the church I had started seven years previously, the church I had poured my life into, and tell the people I loved that I was leaving. I still remember the stunned looks on their faces. Total silence, disbelief and a sense of shock greeted my words. I thought my family and I would be at the Net for life but now God was clearly calling us on to something new. But it was hard to explain this as I looked at people whose lives I knew so well. Many of them had become Christians with us. We had helped people through bereavement, unemployment, divorce and much more. We had experienced with them the highs and lows of their lives. I choked back the tears as I explained what we were doing and many of them had tears rolling down their cheeks as they listened. I tried to help their panic and assure them the church would thrive and flourish. If it was only built on me, then we had failed spectacularly, I told them, but I was confident that its foundations were far more solid than that.

I am writing this almost exactly one year later, sitting in an idyllic Cambridge University college garden on a very warm spring day. It seems a long way from Huddersfield and the creation of a new church. But I wanted to write this book having had time to reflect on what happened and with some distance to enable me to approach the subject a little more objectively.

I would have loved to have called this book *Creating a church made simple, Starting a new church for dummies* or *Five very easy steps for new church* but these are books that would not and could not be written. I'm not suggesting for a moment that if you slavishly follow these precepts, a wonderful church will appear and you will be guaranteed absolute and complete success. I want to emphasise this book is not a blueprint for success. If that is what you want, I'm afraid you've bought the wrong book. This book does not provide you with a flat-pack church which you take out of the box and construct by following the instructions. I simply offer these Essentials as concepts which I discovered were foundational for creating new church. I hope they might provide you with a helpful framework in whatever you are attempting. I do, though, want to encourage you to think outside of the box; not just to follow familiar patterns and ideas, because that's the way we always have done things. There is no secret to the idea of 'ten' Essentials but when I counted them up, there were ten!

When I told the Leadership Team at the Net I was writing this book, their first words were 'Tell them how hard it is!' I certainly don't want to glamorise what we have done. Starting the Net has given me some of the most joyous moments of my life but also some of the darkest days I have ever had to face. I have felt at times strained to breaking point and then God has seemed to take me even further on. But I honestly would not have chosen any other path, even if I knew all that was to come. I felt compelled by God and could do nothing else.

That's why the last two essentials are so important. It's no good if doing God's work destroys the work of God in you. So I hope I can share how God kept me sane in the middle of all this. I often get together with other pioneers and am sure my story is not unique but very typical.

I left the Net to take up a new role in Cambridge, training Anglican ordinands to lead churches like The Net and working with the Diocese of Ely to create more new churches. This has also given me time and space to consider what has been happening, not only in Huddersfield but also throughout Britain and overseas. I have been able to leave the church in very capable hands, it is thriving and the new vicar, Nick, is doing a great job.

A few friends of mine have said to me on a number of occasions 'There are so many books coming out on this subject: why do we need yours?' It is a fair question. It has made me think about what makes this book worth writing, not just for me in producing it but also in you reading it.

As I reflected on this, the word that came to mind was 'ordinary'. That may seem a strange word but I think it is important. This is a very ordinary story. It's not set in one of the bright spots of Britain, or in the south, but in very ordinary Huddersfield. It's not the story either of a mega church or a fast growing wonder church but a smallish church which is around a hundred people now. That's important because a recent report has shown that most new churches are about fifty people. Maybe small really is beautiful when it comes to new churches. I hope it might help you in developing something in your situation that feels realistic, attainable and possible or in keeping going in what you are doing to develop something healthy and sustainable.

I hope you can learn from our mistakes! When something is so new it is very difficult to get it right all the time. The Net is and was far from being 'the perfect church' as you will see very clearly throughout the book. The history of this church includes conflicts and problems. All of us involved have made mistakes and learned some hard lessons. But it's often in that school of hard knocks that the best lessons are learnt. I suppose this is the book I wish I could have picked up when we were starting the Net.

I have been thinking about these issues now for about twelve years, not just with the Net but in helping other churches to get started, and in networking with various church leaders. I certainly don't feel I have all the answers but I am clearer on what the questions are. I hope that some of my reflections might help you in your situation. For some of you, perhaps, it may be the inspiration you need to have a go yourself or to keep going in what you are doing

In working on this book I have battled with what kind of language to use to describe churches like the Net. 'Fresh expressions', emerging church', 'new ways of being church' and 'church planting' are some of the current phrases. These can also vary according to denomination and church groupings, with subtle differences between the descriptions, but in this book I have wanted to find an all-encompassing term. I have used the phrases 'creating church' or 'creating new church'. It is not perfect but I think it can apply whether you are within an established church (creating something new) or starting something from scratch like we did in Huddersfield. My desire in writing this is to be as inclusive as possible in my terminology.

There are many people I want to thank as I begin this book. Above all, I want to thank my wife Heather. In many ways this book is hers as well as mine because we saw the setting up of the Net very much as a joint venture. Without her, I would not be the person and leader I am. Also my children Jenny, Holly and Callum, who have been very much part of this adventure.

I can't go much further without expressing my gratitude to everyone at the Net, both present and past people. It has been a privilege and honour to be church with you. I hope you are satisfied with what I write and feel it is a fair representation of what we experienced together. These were the best years of my life so far. There have been plenty of ups and downs but I have never regretted what we have achieved together. I could name you all but you know who you are. Thank you from the bottom of my heart.

Thank you to all those people who have given me help and advice along the way in the last few years. Your input has been invaluable and I hope you feel it wasn't wasted. I want particularly to thank George Lings, your friendship and advice has been a life saver at times. Thanks also to the lads of the Kingfisher group, or whatever we are called now: your prayers, support and advice have often seen us through big decisions. Thank you to the people in Wakefield Diocese who believed in me enough to back my crazy plan, especially Nigel McCulloch, John Holmes, Richard Inwood and David James. Thanks to Neal and Gill for port and cheese when things got too much. For the people of St Christopher's and Kirkheaton: thanks for letting me learn with you. Thank you to my colleagues here in Cambridge, for all I have learnt from you as I have reflected on the last few years. Thank you to the various pioneer students in Cambridge for your ideas and inspiration and for all those fantastic post lunch discussions.

Thanks to all my friends who have been there for me, especially those who have been there for many years like Alan and Joyce, Dave and Jan and Amanda and Gavin.

Heather's story

I was very excited when Dave came home to tell me we were going to be able to start the Net, but I also felt an overwhelming responsibility. I didn't want to let us, or friends or the Diocese down. If I'm honest, I was fearful of whether we could do it. Working together so closely, especially in the first few years, was very intense, and the church always seemed to be at the forefront of our minds and conversation. Our whole life was geared towards it. It was great that we were so united in our thinking, I think we grew closer together through all that was happening, but we certainly had to work on our boundaries, such as not discussing church stuff during family time or on days off. I found it harder than Dave did to switch off, especially if there were stressful problems with people in the church.

There were some good things: I grew spiritually so much during this time as we were dependent on God and out on a limb. I loved the great sense of community and the unparalleled deep relationships. It was a privilege seeing people come to faith, especially people who would not have set foot in their local church. Some of these were my friends and workmates. I also got excited seeing people grow in their new found Christian faith. But there were also some hard things: I went to most services with my stomach churning, worried about what people would make of what was happening that day. I always found criticism from people within the church hard to handle. Conflict was always tough to deal with and some of it could be very personal. Whenever people chose to leave the Net, it affected me very deeply, and I always wondered if I could have done more.

If I had my time over again, I would definitely do it again, even with all the difficulties. But for anyone starting out on the same path, I would say, 'Be very clear about what God is calling you to do and do not be diverted from that.'

To my Mum, who set me in the right direction. Lastly, thanks to John Clarke, James Bloice Smith, Chris Hancock and the Holiday Club team, who gave a young boy the chance to hear about Jesus and in the next ten years gave me a passion for those outside the church and my first experiences of leadership. It just shows you never know what seeds you might be planting for the future in a ten year old.

The beginning

Three significant meetings

The beginnings of the Net were built around three meetings: one with a stranger in a jacuzzi, another with some Americans at a conference and finally an interview with an Anglican Bishop. It is amazing how God is at work when you are not expecting it.

Meeting one

'What do you actually do, apart from doing a service on Sunday?'

I never ever expected God to plan a life-changing moment when I was in a jacuzzi! Yet a simple question from a total stranger had the most profound impact on me. When the young man got in the jacuzzi, my heart sank. I simply shut my eyes and hoped he would read the social signals. I'd had a hard session in the gym and wanted to chill out. He didn't, though, and we started chatting. Our conversation soon turned to work. I didn't want to be stereotyped but I had to confess I was a vicar and this was swiftly followed by his question. Before I could tell him about the wide variety of my work, he answered his own question, 'I suppose you do things like cleaning the church.'

This was my eureka moment. It struck me with real force that, apart from leading Sunday services, he couldn't think of one useful thing a church or its leader could do that might have any impact on his life or anyone else's. The best we could do was keep the place spick and span! Is this what we have reduced the community of God's people to? Have we somehow changed from disciples of a living active Jesus into curators of a religious building?

As I left the gym that day, all I could think about was that I wanted to be part of a church that is relevant to people like him. Was it possible to create a community that made sense to him? Wouldn't it be incredible if he could find somewhere where faith could seem real and alive? I didn't know what to do with these thoughts but I knew I had to do something. That brief encounter had encapsulated all my frustrations with church. It had also ignited a desire in me to discover if there was some other pattern for church. I was not the same person who had entered the gym ninety minutes earlier. Something had to change or I was going to burst.

I saw the guy a few more times around the gym. Then he left and I have never seen him again. But I am truly grateful for that encounter.

Looking back, I can see how many things had prepared me for that moment. I found I had a growing frustration with the way we did church. I had been involved in small inner city churches and large suburban churches but the issue was always the same. It was unrelated to geography, social standing or numbers. They were great churches full of good people. We were involved in lots of excellent activities and I enjoyed the Sunday services. The real problem which constantly frustrated me and many others was that we struggled to connect with people outside the Church. This issue has become so urgent simply because those outside the Church have become the majority of the population! Yet we continue as though *we* are the majority and that people who don't come to Church are just waiting to flock back. We need to wake up to this new reality. We have to become a missionary church or shrivel and die. We were good at doing church for ourselves but struggled to make any impression on those outside. They just wandered by. The vast majority of these people might have some spiritual questions but mostly they were apathetic about church. What use is this institution for, apart from being another building to keep clean?

About sixteen years ago, I left theological college full of ideas of how God would use me to convert the world. But then reality hit. It wasn't as simple as I thought.

Meeting two

Two years later, I was at a conference on evangelism and we were told there was a lunchtime meeting with some people from America. I went along thinking 'Here we go again, Americans telling us how to do it.' My expectations were severely limited. But for the next forty five minutes, I was blown away by the presentation I heard. Finally, here was a church ruthlessly committed to prioritising people outside the church. I was so excited as I heard them speak. There was hope and, more than that, I had a model to begin from. These people were from Willow Creek Church in Chicago and they told us about the phenomenal growth of their church. But instead of being put off by their success story, I discovered what they said suddenly brought clarity to my thinking. It was as though they had taken my jumbled thoughts, stirred up by a growing sense of frustration and helplessness, and put them into some coherent order. This was the moment when my thinking about church began to develop into something that was definable and tangible. I went home from that conference thinking I wasn't so mad after all. I resolved to find out all I could about this church in Chicago. Over the next few years Willow Creek held many conferences and I devoured their resources.

I came back from that conference a changed person. I talked to some people in my church about what I had heard and we all agreed we had to do something. Eight of us decided to start a monthly service in a local pub, focused on those outside the church. I think the landlord thought I was mad when I asked to hire his function room to hold a church service! On the first Sunday in the month we had great fun creating an event using music, drama, computer graphics, videos and talks. We looked at issues from stress to astrology, from David Beckham to *The Simpsons*. I fondly remember performing a dance to a Spice Girls song and dressing up as a chicken for a sketch! I learnt so much from this experience that would be invaluable in the future. But after two years we pulled the plug on the event. Non Christians were certainly coming regularly but the church was not really behind what we were doing. It felt like tokenism. Most importantly, we realised it was too big a step from what was happening in the pub to our normal church services, lively as they were. The problem wasn't the message but the cultural gap was too wide. Something far more all-encompassing was needed. It wasn't enough to add on a multi-media service in a local pub to what we were already doing. The changes needed to be more fundamental.

Meeting three

The next piece of the jigsaw fell into place a couple of years later in September 1996. I had my annual review with the Bishop. I duly went along and we talked about various matters. Eventually we talked about my future, as it was time to move on from my current position. He pointed out to me two vacancies at the kind of church that he thought might suit me. I was absolutely horrified. I'm sure that they were good churches but they were not the kinds of places that I felt fitted my gifts or calling. I made it plain to the Bishop there was no way I was going to either of them! Exasperated with me and probably in frustration, he blurted out, 'What do you want to do, then?'

This was my moment. Looking back, I can see that God was at work. Everything that had happened to me over the last few years, from the Willow Creek folk to the guy in the jacuzzi, and a myriad of other thoughts, conversations and experiences, had led me to this moment. 'Well', I began, 'what I really want to do is to try and create a church that would connect with people outside the church.' God was in this, because this Bishop didn't put me down as a misguided hothead. His first words to me were, 'That sounds interesting, tell me more.' For the next twenty minutes, I told him of my dreams. We agreed that if there was one place in the Diocese it might work, it would be Huddersfield. This was because of the size and the geography of the place. We finished our meeting with him saying to me, 'Go away and draw up a job description and we will see what we can do.' As I left that room, I realised for the first time that this might really happen.

But it wasn't easy or quick from there. From that meeting with the Bishop it took a further two years before the final decision was taken to start this new church. It was a long time, but this was after The Nine O'clock Service debacle in Sheffield, when a new church had gone horribly wrong. There was a strong sense of institutional nervousness about anything new. Also they were starting to cut ministers' posts because of financial restraints, so how could they justify creating something totally new? I suppose it gave me time to revise my job description. I felt at times that I was trapped in a nightmare of endless committees, meetings and discussions with every conceivable church dignitary.

I thought the church was going to be agreed at a committee meeting in September 1998. How wrong I was. Instead I was sent out from that meeting to talk to even more people. Some were fretting over the money involved. One person at the meeting said, 'But what if they then want a church like this in Wakefield and Halifax, how will we afford it!' All I could think was 'Wouldn't that be a fantastic problem to have!' On the way home, I stopped for a drink at a pub with my wife, Heather. We were both very depressed, wondering if the Diocese would pull back at the last moment. Yet we were sure there was nothing else we wanted to do with our lives. We even talked about her working full-time while I set up the church, without any pay from the Diocese. Money was not going to stop us. I went to bed that night crying out to the Lord to do something and to do it soon.

I was woken that morning at 6am by a phone call from Trevor, a good friend. What made this unusual was that he was in Hong Kong on business, hence the early hour of his call. He told me that he was ringing to see how the meeting had gone. Before I could tell him my woes, he said to me, 'I keep meaning to tell you I want to give you twelve thousand pounds to help with the start of the church.' All I then heard him saying was, 'Dave, Dave are you there?' I was crying too much to say anything. God was confirming to me within seven hours that he had a plan for this church-in-waiting. I must also state categorically that without the support of some key people in the Diocese, I would never have got this far and I will be eternally grateful to them.

Finally, on Thursday 28th November 1998, I went to the meeting at Wakefield Cathedral where my fate would be decided. It was confirmed that the final decision would be made during the meeting, one way or the other. I realised the enormity of the next hour. These eighteen people on the Bishop's Council held my life in their hands. What made it so scary was that I had no Plan B. If this wasn't approved, what would I do? I was a hundred per cent sure this was all I wanted to do.

Despite the impact of their decision upon my family, my future and myself, I was not allowed to speak at the meeting. Permission was granted for me to sit in the room as they discussed my dreams. After fifteen minutes' discussion, they came to the vote. At this point I was expecting them to ask me to leave the room. But they didn't. All I could do was sit and watch helplessly as my future was played out in front of my eyes. Those in favour, those against, abstentions. I held my breath. Then I realised it had gone through and it had gone through unanimously. I decided a massive scream of utter delight and total relief was probably not the thing to do at such a meeting. They had many more agenda items, so I was ushered out into the cold night air. No one said anything to me, apart from good night. As I drove back from that meeting, it hit me that what I had hoped for, for so long, was really going to happen. I had a new church; an embryonic church that I hoped could connect with those outside the church. The only slight problem was at the moment it consisted of me, my wife Heather, and my three children, Jenny, Holly and Callum. What now?

Diocesan Missioner, Wakefield Diocese: John Holmes's story

As Diocesan Missioner in Wakefield Diocese, I was part of the Bishop's staff team which decided on the Net's viability. After it started, I was a member of the church's Advisory Group until my retirement in June 2007.

Why were we prepared to consider this proposal, to start a new church? Bishop Nigel had declared Wakefield Diocese to be a 'missionary diocese' so we were willing to look at new and different ways of being a missionary church. Dave was a credible advocate for this idea because of his past work in the Diocese. To put it bluntly, he and Heather were people we had confidence in.

There were four main factors, for me, in the development and growth of the Net.

Firstly, Dave had a good core of people with him, and with them he developed careful and prayerful plans for the future. Secondly, he worked hard at developing the community life. Thirdly, he received lots of help from the wider church, from some people in particular. He had strong support from them and he knew it. Finally, he was good at doing evangelism through a relational style.

The church developed very much in the way I thought it would, for the first four or five years. There were lots of new people and it was very exciting. Naively I thought this growth would continue unabated. But I think I underestimated how hard it is to build a Christian new community in today's culture. It is a long and difficult journey which is incredibly challenging. I am critically aware you really need perseverance, a long view and really good backing.

The Leadership Team was absolutely critical on this journey together into an unknown territory. One person cannot do it on their own! There must be a group of leaders. The Leadership Team was vital in dealing with relationship problems, policy issues and keeping the church relevant. The need to be constantly creative meant Dave needed gifted leaders who could see the big picture.

As far as the Diocese is concerned, our eyes were opened to another way of doing things. For some it confirmed our hopes and it challenged those who doubted the whole thing. It was working and making a difference and we could all see it.

Essential One

Team

The need for a team chat works

It is important to realise there are different starting places for new churches and there is no one way of proceeding. Some new churches start with one person or a couple, who may feel a calling to a particular area or group and are prepared to start something from absolutely nothing. Many start, like the Net, with a small group of people which could number anywhere between three and fifty people. A few churches start with a larger group.

The numbers you begin with have implications for the life of the church. As a general rule the smaller the starting team, the longer it will be to grow the church. It will take much longer to make and develop contacts and grow to a critical mass. But the bigger the team, the harder it is for those people to adapt to a different culture. A bigger team is more likely to set up a church they like, rather than asking what kind of church they need to be for those who don't attend at the moment. Also the bigger the team, the more likely are team problems, which suck the energy from the main focus of creating church in a new situation.

The role of the team is vital in creating a good start. If a team works well, the impact can be amazing. This is often described as 'synergy', where a group can do more together than the separate parts could do alone; the whole is greater than the sum. But there can also be teams that do not achieve their potential. Dr R.M. Belbin coined the phrase 'the Apollo Syndrome' to describe a group of highly intelligent people who could not perform well as a team for a number of reasons.[1] The main one is that they are always trying to outdo each other, rather than cooperating. For them, the parts are greater than the whole. We wanted to create the right kind of teamwork that would enable God's mission to flourish.

Jesus knew the importance of team. He didn't go it alone but poured himself into twelve others to help him accomplish God's mission. It wasn't easy for that team, though. Even one of Jesus' team didn't make it to the end.

I sat at my desk in our attic room on January 2nd 1999, looking round the room. I was thinking, 'This is the first day of a new church and what do I do now? I have no buildings and no people.' All my training had prepared me to lead existing churches: all my energies had been spent in getting us to this point of getting permission to do this. But where did I start? I honestly didn't know what to do. I made myself a coffee.

I soon realised I could not do it alone. This was a theme which would repeat itself many times. I needed to recruit a team to begin this adventure with us. But how do you do that? The church I had left said that we could take twenty people with us from the congregation, but one or two of the leaders were very worried about this. They were concerned that we 'would take the cream of the church' as they put it to me. I could understand this but this was a church with about three hundred adults! How could taking twenty people wreck the church? The vicar was very nervous about the whole thing. It was probably a generational issue; he was twenty years older than me.

He couldn't see why we needed different types of churches; I couldn't see how churches could remain the same and survive into the future. We talked about this for some time and finally he agreed to the plans.

So began a process of finding those twenty people. Initially we had two large meetings, which we invited anyone from the church to attend. At these, we set out why we felt called by God to create something new in Huddersfield and stressed our vision to connect with those outside the normal orbit of the church. This was a great way of informing people of what was going on and, at the end of each meeting, we suggested if anyone wanted to talk about being involved, they should make contact with us.

Over the next few weeks, we talked to so many people. My wife Heather and I had countless meals and cups of coffee and tea with all sorts of individuals. Our main concern was not their gifts and abilities but whether they felt called by God to this and if they fully supported our vision for the church, to reach people far outside the church. Some people we talked to we knew very well, some were good friends and others we hardly knew at all.

It was important that the team was not solely made up of our friends or choices but that it was the team God wanted. We had to create space for the Holy Spirit to work and create surprises for us. We did suggest to a couple of people that they should think about joining us. These were people who we felt were most in tune with what we were trying to achieve. But generally we tried to avoid engineering the team.

After our discussions, some people came back to us and said they decided it wasn't for them. This was often due to the life stage they were at. For example, one couple felt they shouldn't be moving churches because their children had just settled into a new children's group at the church. Some people we expected to join us; others were people we would never have dreamt of recruiting. There were a couple of people the church was glad to see leave but we believed God was in it and those people were fantastic with us and were undoubtedly God's people for the Net.

As we reflected on this process later, Heather and I were amazed to find that in all the decisions people made, we agreed one hundred per cent with them. Wonderfully, we did not have to say to anyone that they could not come with us. It was remarkable to see God at work in what seemed such a messy process. It was also exciting to talk with so many people about their passion for God, his mission and their part in it.

As we had all these various meetings, I had not kept track of numbers. After a month of talking and people agreeing to join us or not, I reckoned up the numbers on the back of an old envelope. I said to Heather, 'It's amazing: we have twenty adults exactly. Surely God has to be in that.' It was wonderful that God had been in such control.

But we had wanted to start with thirty adults if we could. Initially we hoped that other Anglican churches in Huddersfield would release individuals to join us. After a couple of meetings, I realised this was not going to happen. So we recruited on a wider basis and God provided another eight adults. It was staggering how we came across people, often through random meetings. Some we met through mutual friends. One woman joined after meeting up with an old friend who was joining our team. He had become a Christian in our previous church. Her faith had gone cold but through various conversations with him and his excitement about God, her relationship with God was reignited and she joined us.

Our criteria for those wanting to join the team were simple. Firstly, did they feel called by God to join us and did they share our vision of reaching those outside the church? Secondly, did Heather and I feel they were called by God to this? Thirdly, did their church also feel this and were they willing to send them to join us? If all these answers were positive, then we were happy to have them join us.

As people agreed to join us, we encouraged them to carry on attending their churches but we began meeting together on a Tuesday evening to pray, plan this new venture and get to know each other. We started these gatherings on Tuesday 2nd February 1999 with about ten people attending. Meeting in our lounge, we sat around discussing the possibilities with a growing excitement. As people joined us officially, we asked them to make a commitment to the church by signing up to four commitments:

1. To the vision and aims of the church.
2. To making relationships with God, family and each other a priority.
3. To develop real and relevant relationships with non Christians.
4. To support the church financially.

We wanted people to be clear about what they were doing so we all knew what was expected of us.

At our first meeting, I asked people, 'What are you most excited and most nervous about?' There was a few moments' silence. Then one of the team said, 'It's the same answer to both questions. It's having a blank piece of paper. It's exciting to start from nothing but also very, very scary.' That broke the ice and everybody agreed they felt exactly the same, including me. It was wonderful to have the luxury of starting with a blank canvas. It's much harder to change an existing church. I have seen so many times how this has led to upset, factions, splits and the end of the minister. But it's not easy starting from nothing because you have to create everything. There is real pressure in that.

As we started to meet I knew this had to be our church and not just mine if we were to succeed. I didn't want to have made all the decisions before people joined. They had to feel a real sense of ownership. So over the next two months, on Tuesday evenings, we discussed the vital issues of the name of the church, our vision statement and our values.

We couldn't go on being the church with no name. I asked people to think about possible names and they came back with various ideas. We decided we didn't want a usual church name. My personal idea was C2, with its play on words: this was a new kind of church but it was church too. People thought it was too contrived. Then, in the middle of our discussions, Heather suddenly said, 'What about calling it the Net?' There was a moment's silence and then a murmur of approval. She explained how it combined a number of facets about the church: 'We want to work through networks of relationships, it echoes Jesus' words about being "fishers of people"and it also relates to the Internet, which we want to take advantage of.' There were some reservations that it might give the impression of being 'caught in the net' with all its negative connotations for a church. But in the end we decided the Net was our name. I don't think we ever regretted that decision for a moment. The Net was here to stay.

During those Tuesday evenings, we started the process of dealing with four important issues that all new churches face.

1. What are we doing?

Any book about creating teams will tell you having a common purpose is essential to any team's success. This is such a vital matter that the next chapter will be devoted to it. Many of those first meetings were devoted to defining and refining our common purpose. We had to work this out together and it was not something I imposed on the group. We spent five weeks working on a vision statement on which we could agree and which would propel us into the future. I am not a detail person so discussions over a particular word or phrase were not easy for me. But it was worth it to create an agreed form of words around which we could unite. Finally we emerged with, 'By knowing and loving God and by knowing and loving each other we seek to enable non-churched people to develop a real and relevant relationship with Jesus.'

2. Who is doing this?

As we started to meet together, we soon realised that we had a very talented bunch of people who possessed many different gifts. We were committed to harnessing those. I was fed up with church where roles were filled by guilt, where the leader says, 'If no one signs up to help with the children then we will not be able to have any groups for them.' This did not seem to be about using people's talents. We followed some material which helped to identify and develop people's gifts and initially, people were involved in one of three areas:

Staff

I was employed full-time to work for the church. As we were trying to connect with people in their twenties and thirties, we soon realised that provision for children was important. I'm not sure we ever planned to employ someone to do this but the children's worker from my previous church was available for a year. Helen was great at this work and wanted to work two days a week before training as a physiotherapist. We decided we would employ her for a year and would pay for her through people's giving in the church. So we had a staff team and I had a colleague, and over the years, God seemed to suddenly provide the right person at the right time rather than our working out a rigorous plan.

Leadership Team

After the first few weeks, I realised we could not keep making all the decisions on a Tuesday night. It was not the best use of our time. We were planning a weekend away and it would be mad for all twenty eight of us to plan the intricacies of this together. We also needed to make financial decisions and there were some pastoral issues to deal with. Our time could easily be filled with making detailed decisions and policies. I didn't want to make these decisions on my own, though. We needed some kind of leadership team to lead us in living out our vision as a new church. I wasn't sure how this team should look or who should be on it. We talked about it as a whole church and everyone agreed we needed some type of leadership. Someone pointed out was that we didn't know each other very well and so it was very hard to elect people to the leadership team.

I asked for one year's grace from the church so I could appoint four people to lead the church with me for that time. I assured them that part of our role would be to work out how, in future, we would select and elect members of the leadership team as a whole church. This proposal was unanimously agreed by the church and I chose four people to help me lead the church. Two had leadership experience and two were new to such a position. I thought not only about whether they could do the job but also if they had the right characters. I was also clear I did not want a representative team, for example someone from the children's work, small group work etc: I wanted people with leadership gifts whom God had called to lead the church.

Teams

We needed to create some ad hoc groups to look at specific issues in the church's life. Firstly, we appointed a group to develop the values of the church. Four people volunteered to do this, feeling this would be an area in which they could use their gifts. Their aim was to create a document which laid out the values behind what we were doing.

A second team looked at how we developed our small groups. With our emphasis on both community and evangelism, small groups were important to us. Again two people with a real passion for this, Justine and my wife Heather, volunteered to examine these issues and to return to the whole church with some proposals. They spent three months talking to church leaders, attending a couple of conferences on small groups and reading any literature they could get their hands on. They produced two proposals for the future of small groups which we discussed at a Tuesday night meeting and finally one was agreed upon.

A third team worked with Helen, developing our children's work. The twenty eight adults who started the church came with sixteen children, the oldest being twelve. It was important that our children's activities were not a holding job till they were eighteen but that the children shared the same vision and values as the rest of us. They needed to think about how they could connect with their unchurched friends as individuals and a group. Our vision and values needed to apply to every age in the Net.

Decision-making

We had to make decisions and get going on what God had called us to. We were all involved in the process so there was a sense of shared ownership. But we could not all be involved in every decision or we would never get very far.

Management gurus say there are three options for decision-making, all of which we used in those first few months:

Closed decisions

These are made by an individual or a few people, with no reference to others. Sometimes for specific reasons we did this, for example when Heather and I chose the original team or when I selected the initial leadership team. Sometimes for good reasons this has to be done but it should not be the norm: it soon de-motivates the whole team and makes people feel excluded.

Consultant decisions

These are decisions where people are consulted but a particular person or group makes the final decision. This was the way we developed our values. It is important to give that person or group authority to make decisions after listening and responding to others' views, but it's also important that people feel involved in the process.

Consensus decisions

These are decisions in which everyone is equally involved in the final decision. This process created our vision statement. For some critical decisions you need to ensure that the outcome is worked out by everyone. You can't do this for every decision or church life would grind to a halt. Churches vary in their balance of using these three ways of making a decision. You need to think about the way you make your decisions and its implications for the church.

3. How do we do this relationally?

At the Net we felt that our relationships with each other were as important as what we did together. Heather and I had been deeply impacted by meeting David and Theresa Ferguson from America (more on this in Essential 6).

Even though the majority of us were from one church, we didn't know each other well which made it hard to develop community quickly. So we set about remedying this problem. We spent more time on a Tuesday evening simply getting to know each other better. We worked through material from David Ferguson to help us think what it really meant to love each other and those outside the church. We planned a weekend away in Scarborough together as a church in June. This was a really important time of teaching and discussing what it meant to be the

Net but it also gave plenty of time to let relationships deepen. It was so successful that our weekends away became an annual highlight of the church's year.

Those first few weeks were not always easy. Though we were committed to a common purpose we were also very different from each other. There was a mixture of ages, church experience, background, temperament, gifts and outlook. We had to learn to appreciate the differences. It was not always easy, but we were committed to this. And there were casualties. Even in the first few months, two people who had joined decided the Net was not for them and went back to their original church.

4. How do we do this? The task

Through our Tuesday evenings and the work of the various teams, we began to work on what we were doing. On Palm Sunday March 28th 1999, we held our first service together in a renovated mill on the edge of Huddersfield. The previous Sunday we asked the sending churches to commission the people they had given us.

Strangely, for a church that was aiming to reach unchurched people, initially we did not want new people to join us. We needed a few months to get ourselves together before we were 'open for business'. It gave us time to think about our services and to experiment with different teaching and musical styles. The whole time, though, we had in mind what would unchurched people make of this? We started our children's work under the title of Playstations, and our small group system. By common consent we used a cell church type system for our three small groups.

Over the summer we spent time together, talked, plotted, planned, laughed, ate and prayed together. We started to plan for a grand opening and booked the largest suite at Huddersfield Football Club for our launch. We invited all the churches to celebrate with us at the service. We had big discussions about the launch service and decided because of our vision, the service should be aimed at unchurched people. We used lots of multi-media, drama and mime. The Bishop of Pontefract spoke, commissioned the team and officially launched the Net.

It was very scary to hire a room that can hold up to four hundred people when you are a church of less than thirty adults. The day before we panicked and felt that maybe we had done the wrong thing. How embarrassing would it be if only about fifty people turned up? We did not ask people to let us know if they were coming and so we had no idea if anyone would. But it was amazing. On the launch night of Thursday 30th September 1999, we had to delay the start so we could put out extra chairs. Friends, relatives and local churches came to support us. It was a wonderful way to begin. We also had incredible interest from the national media. I was interviewed by many of the national papers and live by BBC *Look North*, just before the service.

The adventure had officially started. Three days later we held our first Sunday service as a newly launched church at a new venue, the George Hotel in the centre of Huddersfield. I can still picture that service in my mind and feel the excitement of the people gathered there. Our doors were now open for business. We wanted to connect with people who, we believed, were hungry to hear the good news about Jesus. We only stayed at the hotel for a few months because we were quickly growing in numbers so it became unsuitable. We began 2000 having to move across the road to some rooms at Huddersfield University.

Helen's story

I joined the Net because Dave twisted my arm... Seriously, I didn't see myself as part of this new church, because I didn't really believe I was an evangelist. I felt I didn't have much to contribute therefore to this new venture. But Dave talked to me and saw potential in me. I remember bashing this out with him, sitting at his long breakfast bar. I was wondering if I really had what was needed to be part of this. But gradually I became convinced God was leading me to join. Eventually I ended up working for this new church two days a week, leading the children's work.

The first year was mixed but not in a bad way. It was very hard work but it was also an adventure. It felt like we were always trying something new and that was good. It was scary but great building something from scratch. It was certainly novel to be involved in naming a new church!

It was great getting to know each other. When we used to meet on a Tuesday night to work on our vision and values, I felt we were very inclusive. Everyone was involved and their views and ideas counted. The highlight was being in something with other people that had a real drive and purpose. Also some of our celebrations as a church family were great fun and really meaningful to me. After my fears about joining the church the Net has taught me how to relate to my non-Christian friends and to give a priority to them. The harder things were the relationship problems and people leaving.

I began to understand, the more we worked out together what we were doing as a church, the more it didn't suit everyone.

I could never have done this on my own and God never intended it to be that way. Those first few months were heady times, full of energy and anticipation. It wasn't always easy to manage and I was kept on my toes. But we got this church up to a speed where it could lift off and start to fly.

Over the next few years, as the church grew, the way we operated and organised ourselves had to change. We tried to keep the structures light and flexible but, for example, we abandoned our Tuesday nights to meet in a variety of small groups. I think some of the original team yearned for those early days, when we were small and decisions were made all together. We now had to work harder to create social time for the whole church and to ensure our communication was efficient. Growth means change and that takes adjustment, and in the middle of all this we were about to hit our first major crisis (see Essential Three).

Questions for discussion and reflection

1. What were your criteria for joining the team?

2. How is the size of your team impacting what you are doing? What are the advantages and disadvantages of your team size?

3. How do you make decisions and is the balance correct between the varying forms of decision making?

4. Is your team experiencing synergy? If not, can you identify why not?

5. What is the balance between relationship and task for your team? Is this balance about right?

Books

R.M. Belbin, *Management Teams: Why they Succeed or Fail* (Oxford: Butterworth Heinemann, 2003)

B. Hughes, *Leadership Tool Kit* (Eastbourne: Kingsway, 2002)

John C. Maxwell, *The 17 Indisputable Laws of Teamwork* (Nashville: Thomas Nelson, 2001)

Essential Two

Listening

How to listen before acting

When I tell the story of the Net, people are often surprised that, having started as the sole employee of this fledgling church in January 1999, our first public service was not till October 1999. It may seem curious that with all my passion to connect with unchurched people it took ten months to get going.

Yet I am so glad we took our time because we needed to gather the team and to listen. Listening is not my number one skill, as anyone who knows me will tell you, but it is essential for creating new church. In our enthusiasm, we can quickly rush in and get started and that can be foolhardy and dangerous. Listening at the start can prevent some very costly mistakes in the future.

There are two models of creating church that are presently used. The first is the traditional jigsaw model. Creating church here is like doing a jigsaw; it is a matter of putting the right pieces together following the image on the top of the box. We know what it means to create church: as long as we have the right buildings, worship, children's work, preaching, small group system or whatever else we think is important. It will fit together and it must work.

I'm not sure this jigsaw type model is so successful in today's world. There is an inherent danger with it. We think we can move it into different situations and it will always work. I call this our default setting. This is computer speak for the basic position a computer will always take you back to if things go wrong and it's equally true of church life. We all have a default setting and it tends to come out when we are under pressure. Often it is subconscious. It's how we think proper church should be and is often shaped by our past experiences of church, both good and bad. The danger is we try to transport our model elsewhere regardless of the culture, social background or other factors.

The second church model is of a mosaic. Creating church is like a free mosaic made up of lots of broken pieces of ceramic. Sometimes it's difficult to discern exactly what the picture or pattern is. You may have to look at the image for some time to work out what is being depicted. With this model, though, the big difference is that it is not us creating something but God working his purposes out. Our role is to try and discern what he is doing and work with him. I think this is a more biblical model as it reminds us ultimately that this is God's mission and church, not ours. Our role is to co-operate with him in what he is doing. The jigsaw model can give us the impression that we are initiating the work and it depends on how successfully we put all the pieces together. We may need to rethink how we see our task. Tim Dearborn helpfully sets out the changes which need to happen in our thinking. He writes, 'It's not the church of God which has a mission but the God of mission who has a church.'[2] It is God's work and we co-operate with him. It is not our work which we hope God will bless.

So who are we supposed to listen to and what does listening mean for us?

Listening to God

If this is God's mission, then it is important that we listen primarily to God and don't assume we know all the answers. Peter discovered this in Acts 10. I think Peter had an impressive default position for church. The first church of Acts 2 in Jerusalem was not a bad start. It was amazingly successful by any standards as Luke reminds us, 'And the Lord added to their number daily those who were being saved'(Acts 2:47). It is often used as a blueprint for church today. I sometimes hear people say, 'If only we could get back to the church in Acts 2.' I think there is much to be said for this view but, for Peter, it was a dangerous default position. When you have been blessed so obviously by God, it is easy for a previous model to dominate your plans. It would have been natural for Peter to think 'We have our version of church and all we have to do is to roll it out to Judea, Samaria and to the ends of the earth. We know what we are doing and now we just need to export the model across the known world.'

But it wasn't that simple for Peter. He had to listen to God and work out what God was doing. The mosaic, Peter began to discover, was very uncomfortable for him. Suddenly in Acts 10 Peter had a vision from God of a huge sheet full of every kind of animal and he was told to eat. Now, being a good Jew, he could not do that: some of these animals were ritually unclean. But God was insistent and through this vision made the point that all things were now clean, including the Gentiles. Through Peter's subsequent meeting with Cornelius, a Gentile and a Roman soldier, he understood the significance of the dream and said, 'I now realise how true it is that God shows no favouritism' (Acts 10:34). Peter's default position of a church only for the Jews was blown apart. The good news of Jesus was not limited to the Jews. Church was for all types of peoples.

Our listening to God might not be as dramatic as Peter's but it is vital we are listening to him. Prayer is the foundation of all we do. When we started meeting as a small team on a Tuesday night in our lounge, we spent lots of time praying and being quiet before God. We wanted this to be God's church and not our default position. We must not dive straight into doing before we are sure of what God is calling us to do.

We also asked other people to pray for us and with us, particularly people with intercessory gifts. Initially we sent out regular prayer letters to prayer partners both locally and nationally so they could pray with us. It was a great way to gain support but also to ensure that we were paying attention to God's plans and not just our own.

As well as speaking to God, we tried to listen to what he was saying, both when we were together and in our own personal times with God. For some people this was a new concept. I believe God often wants to communicate with us directly but we are simply too busy to hear from him. The daily Bible reading for February 10th 1999, from UCB's *Word for Today* which three different people read, was significant for the church: 'If you want to catch fish, you've got to go where they are, for they're not going to come and jump into your boat.' We felt it was saying something to us as a church and it was part of the thinking behind our naming the church the Net.

Listening to each other

The people in the team had so much to contribute from their experiences, skills and knowledge. It was important that as the leader I didn't assume I knew everything and that their role was to follow me and agree to my plans. Yes, I had the initial vision but it needed to be a shared vision that we shaped and lived out. It isn't always easy and it can be quicker to go with what the leader thinks or wants to do. But that doesn't help to maintain a long term community. We needed to share in this together, to learn from each other and to work out our disagreements.

Listening to the world

It is important we understand the changes in our society and try to understand what is going on. It would be easy to see this as something very different from prayer. This is the secular bit as opposed to our spiritual stuff. But the Bible suggests that God is involved in both parts. The book of Daniel shows God was not only in charge of Daniel's life but was working out his purposes through the changes in society. The coming of the hated Babylonians was all part of God's mosaic, messy as it seems to us (Dan. 1:1–2).

A changing culture

People often use the term post-modern to talk about our society. This is a very difficult term to define because we are not clear what we are becoming; only what we are leaving behind. We are a society in transition. Robert Warren has described this very helpfully as a process that is taking place but is not true for everyone. He talks of a society in a state of flux, moving from one set of values to another, but with people at different places on this continuum.

Moving from	Moving to
Christendom	Spirituality
Authority	Authenticity
Conforming	Choosing
Community	Self reference
Sunday	Time chaos
Organizations	Networks[3]

Not everything in the first column is good, nor is everything in column two bad. Cultural change supports and detracts from the Christian faith.

The biggest change we face is that for the last thousand years the church has been at the centre of our life as a nation but now its influence is fast waning. Callum Browne says, 'What is taking place is not merely the continued decline of organised Christianity but the death of the culture which formerly conferred Christian identity upon the British people as a whole.'[4] There has been a massive cultural shift in the last fifty years which is bigger than simply people not going to church. Browne is saying something more foundational is taking place. The place of the church has shifted from the centre to the margins. People no longer listen to what the church tells them to do and the church's role at the heart of society is continually being diminished. When Tony Blair was asked if he prayed with George Bush during a *Vanity Fair* interview, Alastair Campbell allegedly quickly intervened to say, 'We don't do God here.' That sums up the public role of faith. It is still acceptable to believe but it's a private thing: you must not impose it on anyone else. More and more of the church's role in public life is being eroded. I heard a Bishop say recently that it's very hard to say anything to the media because his views are immediately downgraded because they are seen as coming from someone with a religious perspective. He is seen as biased and not therefore worth listening to. This means that we no longer hold a privileged position in society and people will not listen to us or come to us just because we are the church. On the positive side it means we have to work at being authentic and we have to earn our place to be heard amongst many other competing voices.

These changes in our society have relegated the church to the margins and will affect the way we will have to do church in the future. A number of factors are having an impact on us:

Changing Sundays

We now have competition from shopping, leisure activities and sports. When I was young, little happened on a Sunday, apart from church. The shops were closed and there were very few organised activities. But now Sunday is like any other day of the week. The shops are open most of the day and sometimes night, people play sports on a Sunday, and there are lots of other organised activities. Many more people have to work on a Sunday. Forty per cent of families with dependent children have at least one parent who works regularly at the weekend. So it may not be possible for people to attend a church service at 10.30 am on a Sunday morning, even if they want to go. It's also not as simple as finding a different time to meet. In our 24/7 society, there is no longer one time which is free and therefore ideal for meeting together. You will never find a time when everyone is free to be at church. Believe me, we have tried to find that time and it no longer exists!

Changing relationships

The way we relate to each other has also undergone a transformation. In previous generations, relationships were based around family and geography. These factors are no longer constant. Our home, work and social life are often no longer in one small geographical area. Our increasing mobility means many people may live in one place, work many miles away and be part of clubs, groups and societies elsewhere. This is often referred to as the 'network society'. We now choose the networks that we are part of. For some, we don't even need to leave home. The Internet creates community across all geographical barriers. The rise of sites like My Space and Facebook means that we can create virtual communities that exist to bring people together.

The old static picture of community is changing rapidly in many areas, though not all. Ulrich Beck sums this up when he says, 'to live in one place no longer means to live together and living together no longer means living in the same place.'⁵ I find it interesting that church leaders still talk about their local area and many churches still work exclusively within a particular geographical locality. But this ignores the way that many people live their lives. I was working with one church in the Midlands who told me that many of the people on their estate leave on a Monday morning and don't come back till Friday evening. They then go off for the weekend to visit friends and relatives all over the country. What does it mean to be the local church in that situation?

Changing religious views

You would think from the media that we have become a much more secular nation. But that is simply not true. We are still very much a spiritual people but we no longer define this in terms of Christianity. In some recent research by David Hay and Kate Hunt, 38 per cent of people interviewed admitted an awareness of God's presence (up from 27 per cent in 1987), 37 per cent admitted receiving help in prayer (up from 25 per cent in 1987) and 25 per cent admitted an awareness of the presence of evil (up from 12 per cent in 1987).[6] The majority of people do believe in something out there but do not have a well formed and coherent view of a personal God. Sixty-seven per cent of people in Britain believe in God today but only 25 per cent believe in a personal God.[7] We often see some of this incipient spirituality being expressed at national moments, such as the death of Princess Diana or the Dunblane shootings. The problem is that the church is no longer the place people look to in order to express their longings or to seek answers for their spiritual questions. I met a student last week who told me she was very interested in the meaning of life and had found the answers on the Internet, in astral planes and spiritual powers. People are increasingly attracted today to Eastern philosophies, Chinese medicines, alternative therapies, paganism, inner self-awareness and many other practices which make up what is often referred to as the New Age. People often say to me that they are not religious (by which they mean they are not churchgoers) but they are spiritual. And there are the various religions which are now part of our multi cultural society such as Islam, Hinduism and Buddhism. The church's previous monopoly on faith has now long gone; we now are in a competitive market with very few in built advantages for the church.

Changing generations

We are much more aware now of the difference between generations. Sociologists have given different names to various generations, such as Baby Boomers, (born 1946–1963), Generation X, (born 1963–1978) and Generation Y (born 1978–2000). The dates for these generations are not exact and tend to be defined slightly differently by various writers. Whatever we make of such categorisation, it does help us to see that the generations have different priorities, purposes, hopes and aspirations. This means they want and expect different things from church. It is very difficult to do sixty minutes on a Sunday and connect with all of them.

All these changes have had an impact on who goes to church and who is even interested in going to church. Some fascinating research was done by Leslie Francis and Philip Richter.[8] It looked at why people stopped going to church. They discovered that approximately 10 per cent of the adult population attended church regularly, while a further 10 per cent attended occasionally, often coming to church at Easter, Harvest or Christmas. This second group are often called the fringe. Forty per cent had stopped going to church. This group have been called the dechurched. They could be further subdivided: half of them drifted away from church but would be open to returning if they met up with the right people or church. Classically these might be people who had moved house but had never got back into church going and simply lost the habit. It wasn't a conscious decision to stop going, it just somehow slipped away over time. The other half had made a deliberate decision to leave church and would not consider going back. They might have left because they had fallen out with the minister or someone in the congregation. A student of mine nicknamed this group the dischurched.

Many of this dechurched group went regularly to Sunday school. So much of our previous evangelism has been reconnecting people with their childhood faith. But that inheritance we have been living off is rapidly diminishing. In 1900 55 per cent of children attended Sunday school but by 2000, the figure was 4 per cent.

Finally, 40 per cent of adults have never had any contact with a church, apart from maybe going to a wedding or funeral. This group is often referred to as the unchurched.

Recently Tearfund have done some research in the same area.[9] They polled seven thousand adults for their research, whose findings suggest 15 per cent of the population attend church at least monthly and 10 per cent are fringe people. But 66 per cent of adults have no connection with church (or any other religion). This group is evenly split between the dechurched and unchurched. Of this two thirds of the adult population, only 6 per cent were open to accepting an invitation to go back to church as they have previously known it or understood it. This is a big decrease from the 20 per cent of the Richter and Francis study.

As the Tearfund report states, 'The secular majority presents a major challenge to churches. Most of them are unreceptive and closed to attending church; churchgoing is simply not on their agenda.' We need firstly to acknowledge that we are no longer the majority and we cannot return to a time when the church was central to our society. We are truly in a missionary situation. Previously we sent people off to far flung places to evangelise people, now we have to learn how to do it in our own nation. Unchurched people are not going to present themselves at the church door. So how do we connect with them? We are much more experienced at working with the fringe and dechurched groups. Our services, groups and evangelism connect with them because they understand our language, concepts and ways of operating.

The changes in our culture force us to consider what we are doing and prevents us from reverting to our default position or reinventing church as it previously was. As we thought about these issues at the Net, as we considered the figures, as we prayed over all the issues we faced, we felt called to create a church that would connect with unchurched people. As we were thinking about these issues, I saw in the local paper statistics which suggested 53 per cent of people had no contact with any religious institution in Huddersfield. These were the people we felt called to. Many people asked me 'Why are you starting another church in Huddersfield when there are already too many?' They were right, but we did not want to fill the Net with people from existing churches, but to become a place where unchurched people, with no church experience, could find relevant answers to their questions about life and faith.

We were even more specific than just wanting to connect with unchurched people. We felt called particularly to people between 20 and 45 years old, which seemed to be the missing years in the churches in Huddersfield. This didn't mean we asked for some proof of age before people could join the church. But we realised we couldn't reach everyone in Huddersfield, so we had to discover from God what our specific part was in his plan. We were not exclusive about who could come but we needed to be focused.

This led to a further decision about what kind of church we might become. Many people in this age range seemed to be very mobile. They often travelled a distance to work and for their social lives. This led us to create a church that could connect with these people through their networks. We didn't just pick a local geographical locality to operate in but we decided to work across the town and beyond to connect with these people through their networks. We could do this through our friendships, work and social lives which stretched across many geographical locations. We added to this other social networks we could work through, such as sport and the Internet.

Finally we felt that church buildings could be off-putting. So we decided to hire ordinary venues for our meetings such as pubs, hotel function rooms, an art gallery and a café. We realised from our research that Huddersfield was unusual in that it had no out-of-town shopping areas. People still came to the town centre to do their shopping and for much of their social life. We decided to use what was normal for people and so we hired venues in the town centre, within the inner ring road.

These kinds of decisions came out of our listening to God and to what was happening in our society. They did not happen immediately but through our reflections on what we saw happening and what we felt God was calling us to do in response.

Listening to the locality

As well as listening to the big story of what is happening in society, we also need to listen to what is happening in our own locality. We found there were three simple ways to do this.

Watch

Use your eyes. Where do people gather? What are the issues that matter to them? Where are the shops and leisure facilities? What effect does the physical layout of your locality have on it? For example, Huddersfield was unusual in having no out-of-town shopping facilities so the town centre still played a vital role in the life of the place. Do some prayer walking in your area, asking God to help you notice where he might be at work.

If you are working through a network such as youth culture, clubbers, people in a particular work place, the same research principles apply but will need to be done in a slightly different way.

Look

Use your eyes to find and collect material. There is lots of data out there. The census returns available in your local library will give some fascinating statistics concerning your area. They are worth patient study, as they give important information about age profiles and social groupings. The local paper will also tell you much about what is going on locally. Talk to local church ministers, as they have often gleaned a lot of information over the years.

Listen

Use your ears. I often hear church leaders say 'This is the kind of thing non-Christians would come to.' Sometimes I ask them 'Have you asked any then?' Normally the answer is no. One of the easiest ways to do this is to ask your friends, who are not part of a church, what they think about your plans and ideas. This kind of direct feedback is invaluable.

We did a very simple thing at the Net. We organised an evening at a local pub, provided a buffet and then invited some of our friends to come and tell us what they thought church should be like. One of our church members, who was very skilled at leading this kind of meeting, chaired it. We were clear to everyone present that we were there to listen. This was not an evangelistic meeting but a chance for them to tell us what they really felt. It was important that we didn't interrupt them or tell them why they were wrong in what they thought about church. They were asked about what their impressions of church were; either from going to church or just what they had picked up from the media. Then we explained about how we were hoping to create a church for people who didn't normally go to church and asked them what this new church should look like. What it would need to be like to connect with people like them? In many ways it was a very simple thing to do but it was a very profound listening exercise for all of us.

Some people may feel that some of this research is unspiritual or a waste of time. I believe it is neither but an important beginning to our mission. There are many precedents in the Bible for this kind of preparation, such as Moses sending out spies to the Promise Land, Nehemiah going to examine the broken walls of Jerusalem or Paul discovering more about the spiritual life of Athens (Num 13; Neh. 2:11–16; Acts 17: 16–34).

Listening to other churches

One of the first things I did was to find out if there was any church trying to do similar things to what we hoped to do. There is no point in reinventing something if someone is already doing it. I discovered there was a network church that had already started in Nottingham. I went and met with the leader of the church to find out what they were doing and why. The few hours we had together were so helpful. As he talked about what they were doing, I learnt so much, both positive and negative. The most important thing he said to me was to make a promise to all the local churches that after we had the initial team we would not take Christians from their churches, and if they tried to join us we would send them back. They had done it and found it so important in keeping good relationships with other churches.

That piece of advice was so vital in gaining the trust and support of local churches and reassuring them of what we were about. Even to this day, the Net's website makes clear that if you already belong to a local church, then the Net is not for you {http://www.netchurch.org.uk}. We have sent people back to their churches.

I also learnt some important lessons about what I wouldn't do. These reflections helped me to think about what we might do instead and why. For example, I realised that in the way they organised themselves, there wasn't really a time when all the age groups came together. I felt strongly that it was important we came together regularly as a community of all ages.

When we started the Net, there were not many other churches like us. That's no longer the case. I would urge you to meet up with leaders from new churches to learn from them. I would also encourage you to read as much as you can about what is currently happening, both in the church and in society. The point of all this is not to produce a clone of the latest wonder church but to learn from others' experience and at least save yourself from repeating their mistakes. There is now so much information out there in printed form and on the web to help you.

Those days of listening were vital as we reflected together on what God was saying to us. The information we received, directly or indirectly, helped to inspire and shape our vision and the way the church looked. But this was more than just an information gathering exercise. God also used it to bring us closer together and to inspire and excite us about what might be possible. I still remember those Tuesday evenings in our lounge as we talked and became more and more excited about the possibilities and what God might be able to do through us. These listening exercises were more than preparation; they were the start of our mission and our church as we discovered together the mosaic God was creating. As we glimpsed parts of the pattern he was constructing we felt even more excited and committed to what we were doing.

Finally, it is important to add that listening is not a one-off activity that happens at the beginning of a church's life. This is something we must always be doing. One of the Net's values is being open to change. We wanted to listen continually so that we were always open to further change and adaptation. This is part of what it means to operate with the mosaic model. It means continually being prepared to change as we seek out the patterns God is creating.

Questions for discussion and reflection

1. Do you have a default position of church? What does it look like?

2. How are you listening to God as leaders and a church?

3. Who might you need to listen to? How could you do this?

4. Can you identify the types of people you are trying to connect with?

5. How are the changes in our society impacting your thinking about church?

Books

Steven Croft, *Listening for Mission: Mission audit for fresh expressions* (London: Church House, 2006)

Christian A. Schwarz, *Natural Church Development: A guide to eight essential qualities of healthy church* (St. Charles: Churchsmart Resources, 1996)

Robert Warren, *The Healthy Churches Handbook* (London: Church House, 2004)

Essential Three

Focus

Keeping the main things 'the main thing'

It didn't take long for that crisis to hit us. I remember speaking at our first year anniversary service. There was so much to celebrate, the church growing, people coming to faith. I was talking about all the amazing things that happened in that first year with the rest of the church but inside I was thinking, 'Enjoy this, Dave, because I don't think there will be a second anniversary.' I was convinced the whole thing was about to disintegrate in front of my eyes.

After about only six months of this new church's life, I was aware there were a small number of people who were increasingly unhappy with what was happening in the church. To make it even more difficult, two of these people were on the Leadership Team. In the next few months, I felt that I was clinging on to the church by my finger nails. These individuals no longer liked the way we conducted our worship gatherings, how we viewed the Bible or how we were developing our evangelism. I spent more and more time with them and as I did their impatience with me seemed to increase exponentially. I realised how very fragile we were. The pressure coming upon us made me feel the church would collapse.

Then one Saturday morning I met with one of the people involved to talk again about her feelings concerning the church. I think we both felt very frustrated with each other. I was beginning to believe there was no way out of this downward spiral. But in the middle of our conversation, I suddenly understood the situation. I said to her, 'I'm beginning to realise what's been happening and why we haven't been able to understand each other. Maybe we are working to two different agendas. I am trying to create a church for people who have no connections with church: you want to create a church for people who are in church but are fed up with their present experience of it.' This was a eureka moment for both of us. As we talked more, it helped us see why there had been so many problems: we were working to different agendas. I was able to say that there was nothing wrong with their focus but it wasn't the Net's and at this initial stage we couldn't afford to be working with two visions of the future. As graciously as I could, I explained either they would need to come behind the original focus or they were free to set something up themselves to achieve their dreams.

Unfortunately, over the next few months these people decided to leave the Net. This was a sad event for all of us. It's not easy to lose key people at the start of a new venture. These were people that I had worked with so closely and I cared about them deeply. But I believe it was vital that we stayed focused on our calling from God. We were not at a place where we could or should be diverted from that. At the time it felt like a disaster. It was hard emotionally for all of us to cope with it but I believe it had to be sorted out if we had a future as a church.

Why does a church need a vision statement?

Those horrendous events convinced me that a clear focus is vital for the life of a new church. If you surveyed one hundred people in most churches and asked them what the church was for, you would probably receive a hundred different answers. I find this totally exasperating. It makes it very difficult to develop forward momentum or to determine progress, because we have no idea of where we want to be. It is self evident that if you aim for nothing you will probably hit it! My previous experiences of church made me committed to creating a church where every single person knew exactly what the church was for and therefore what their place in it was.

So when we started the Net, I wanted us all to be clear on what God had called us to do. Business books talk of this as developing vision, which is simply creating a clear sense of where you want an organisation to go and what you want it to be. We had a very strong sense of our direction as we wanted to create a church that would connect with unchurched people in Huddersfield.

But we wanted to have more than a sense of direction. We wanted to define our vision clearly and to put it into words exactly. This process is usually referred to as writing a mission or vision statement. This is a concise statement in which an organisation seeks to identify its primary goals. (It is worth noting that in management books, vision, values and mission often have varying precise definitions.) As you know from previous chapters, this was not something we decided in a few minutes. We spent weeks developing and honing, until we were happy with each word. This statement was vital as it would set our course for the future.

Our vision statement said 'By knowing and loving God and by knowing and loving each other we seek to enable non churched people to develop a real and relevant relationship with Jesus.' It is still the vision statement eight years later.

We wanted to say that our priority was connecting with people outside the church but we also knew that church is more than this. Our priority for evangelism had to come from our relationship with God and each other. It is out of our receiving unconditional love from God, and our developing community with each other, that we are sent out into God's world with love for God and for others. Like many other churches, our vision statement is a bringing together of the Great Commission and Great Commandment (Mt. 22:34–40, 28:16–20).

The working out of your own particular vision is vital as you create something new. It is painting a picture of what you see as your preferred future. I think for a vision statement to work there are some important factors to be considered.

It needs to challenge

It must be something people feel excited and passionate about. It must provide a rallying call that will draw people towards a compelling and exciting future. For us, seeing unchurched people coming to follow Jesus has always been that. We were aware it was not an easy calling but were prepared to make sacrifices to see this come about. I would sometimes paint a picture of God welcoming people into his presence who had become Christians at the Net. 'Imagine', I used to say, 'how you will feel on Judgement Day looking on and thinking to yourself, I have been part of this.' How can we fail to be moved by this?

It needs to be memorable

The danger of many vision statements I have seen is that they are either too long or they are simply banal. Last week, I discovered a church whose vision statement covered eight sides of A4. To be effective, it needs to be three sentences at most. It has to be short enough for all church members to memorise it. It needs to be specific but also create excitement. We could have said we want to be a church that lives out the Great Commandment and Great Commission but that doesn't make a compelling statement. The statement has to energise people for action.

It needs to make sense

A vision statement needs to be realistic as well as challenging. To say you are going to see your whole town become Christians may, in the long run, become a vision that is hard to sustain. If people think this is impossible, they will soon feel deflated. It needs to stretch people and their faith but also be achievable with God's help.

It needs to be lived by the leader

It is vital that the senior leader is more than in agreement with the vision: they need to be seen to be living it out before the church. This is especially important if that person has not been involved in developing the vision statement. If they are not showing by their words and actions they believe in it *wholeheartedly*, then it will be an uphill battle.

It needs to be owned by the church

This may seem obvious but everybody has to want, and be able, to get behind the vision. I once heard a minister give a wonderful talk to his church about a five year plan. But it was obvious, as discussion flowed, that this was his plan and not that of the whole church. Trying to get this vision implemented was going to be an uphill task. The whole church must feel it is their vision, not something imposed on them.

Alongside the vision statement, we developed a set of values which set out how we aimed to live out the vision. Every organisation has values, whether they are aware of them or not. Values communicate messages to both those inside and outside the organisation about what is important and what the priorities are. For example, if you go into a shop, its décor, layout and how you are served will communicate the firm's values to you. It will tell you how highly they prize their customers, what kinds of shoppers they are trying to attract and what they think of their employees. Values do not need to be written down to be in operation: every organisation has them but it does help greatly if the values are acknowledged.

We wanted to be conscious of our values and to live them out as a community. Initially they were worked upon by one of our ad hoc teams. They produced a wonderful set of values for us. The problem, we discovered, was that because they covered two sides of A4 no one referred to them. They were just too full to be either memorable or usable. So we worked on them and boiled them down to seven pithy sayings. They have guided us as we strived to live out our vision. These are the values we distilled to enable us to fulfil our focus. We were to be:

God centred
Our priority was our relationship with God.
Bible-based
Our commitment to the word of God was central to all we do.
Desiring authentic relationships
Our desire was for a developing honesty and reality with each other.
Seeker focused
Our aim was to help people of all ages find Jesus.
Creating relevant faith
Our daily lives and faith needed to be integrated so that we lived out what we believed.
Developing discipleship
Our concern was to help each other grow in our relationship with God.
Open to change
Our principles made us willing to take risks as we sought to follow where God led.

Ironically, sometimes both in emerging church circles and in more traditional churches, the idea of being focused and developing vision statements is not popular. The charge is made that the church has sold out to current business practices. In some new churches I visited in America last summer, having a stated vision was seen as far too directional and dictatorial, too structured and controlling. They would rather that a variety of priorities emerge over time without any strong overarching vision. I think there is a place for a focused approach which is not dictatorial but which creates a framework within which new things can emerge.

There is also a fear that focus takes away the importance of individuals. People simply become targets or figures to be reached. This can be a danger but you can still be focused and treat them as individuals loved by God. The two things are not incompatible. I believe it is fundamentally important to know as a church what you are doing, why you are doing it and what you are aiming for in the future.

It is the way that Jesus and others worked

You cannot read the gospels without seeing that Jesus was focused but not totally task orientated. In Mark's gospel, his mission statement is clear from the beginning: 'The time has come . . . The Kingdom of God is near. Repent and believe the good news!' (Mk. 1:15). He quickly chooses a team to work with. Yet by Mark 1:38 when everything is going so well, he says to the disciples, 'Let us go somewhere else – to the nearby villages – so that I can preach there also. That is why I have come.' In Mark 2:17, after complaints about the company he was keeping, he said, 'It is not the healthy who need a doctor, but the sick. I came not come to call the righteous, but sinners.' Jesus was focused. In Luke 19:10 he said, after his encounter with Zacchaeus, 'For the Son of man came to seek and save what was lost.' He was focused because he was on God's mission and he was committed to seeing this task through. But in the middle of his mission he did not lose sight of the individual. In Mark 5 he is hurrying to help one of the leading people in the community whose daughter is about to die. Then he is touched in the middle of a huge crowd by a woman who had no status in that community. Yet Jesus stopped immediately, healed her, spoke with her and found out who she was.

It is not only Jesus who was focused and painted images of a new future. Moses in the Old Testament had a vision of the future for the people of Israel in the

Promised Land and kept reminding them of it and moving them towards it. Nehemiah was inspired by the vision of rebuilding the broken walls of Jerusalem, while Ezra was focused on the rebuilding of the Temple. In the New Testament, Paul was focused on his apostolic ministry so that churches could be established throughout the known world. I do not think being focused and having a defined vision is either unbiblical or out of date.

It helps you to say No!

One of the biggest dangers when you start a new church is that everyone has ideas about what you should do. I remember within a few months we were inundated with great ideas of what we could or should be doing. Some people said we should be starting a soup kitchen, others were asking if we could start working with youth in the town centre, while yet others wanted to start a mums and toddlers group there. With a small team beginning the church, we couldn't do all these great things. Our vision statement meant we had a way to make decisions. As a leadership team, we were able to ask what helped us fulfil our vision statement and what was possible to do with limited resources.

It also helped us later on in the church's life to think about why we did certain things. When we tried to do something aimed specifically at unchurched people we soon discovered that Sunday morning was far from an ideal time. Sunday evening did not seem much better. It seemed to be the time when people got ready for the next week or wanted to chill out. We discovered that Friday or Saturday evening was the best time for such meetings. But some people felt that we should also meet on a Sunday morning. Theologically, the Leadership Team felt strongly that Friday or Saturday night was our 'Sunday service' or what else were we doing when we met? This was a proper and valid time of worship, even if it didn't look or feel like a normal Sunday. It also emphasised our value of attracting those outside the church that we viewed this as our main activity. Practically we didn't want to exhaust people with extra meetings but wanted to free up time to develop relationships with those around them, again reflecting our values. Under intense pressure from a couple of influential people, I relented on one occasion and we held a prayer meeting on the Sunday morning. As soon as I turned up for the meeting, I knew it was a mistake. Obviously it wasn't praying together that was the problem but the messages it sent out about our priorities and focus. We never did this again, despite some people's protests.

It helps you to change

The vision statement helped us review what we were doing. It prevented us from becoming static and stagnant. Our vision remained constant, to reach unchurched people, but the way we achieved this vision changed over time for numerous reasons. The danger in church life is that we keep on doing the same things, whether they work or not. Church life can easily get into a rut, even for a new church. I have a cartoon in my office of the second ever meeting of a new church and a church member is saying, 'But we didn't do it like that last week.' We were prepared to do or change anything to fulfil our vision.

Three years ago, we picked up grumblings that our small group system was not working well. The groups were running out of energy and the system was too rigid for many people. In our Leadership Team meeting, it took us about thirty seconds to recognise we had to change. We simply asked from our mission statement, 'Are our small groups helping us to love God more, to love each other more and to connect with unchurched people?' We knew immediately the answer was a resounding no. We then spent four months consulting with the church about what they felt we needed to do. We eventually created a number of small groups based around various interests such as discipleship, prayer and meditation, a town centre group for single young adults, a running group, a social action group and a Bible study group. People choose which group to go to. Part of the groups' role was to work out their focus, which reflected the church's vision statement. These new groups were much more successful and flowed with energy.

Recently I was asked by a church near to Cambridge to help them review the new church they have been creating over the last year. Firstly I asked them what they were trying to achieve, beyond putting on a multi-media service. They answered that they were trying to connect with unchurched people. So the second simple question was whether that was happening. They admitted that they had not attracted many unchurched people. It had been great for people on the fringe of church life but very few people with little church connection were coming. So we then talked about whether their focus was the correct one. They still felt it was and so we talked about some things they might be able to do differently to connect with unchurched people. My experience suggests this is not an uncommon scenario for churches to face. New churches start wanting to reach unchurched people and can end up attracting fringe people and disgruntled church members. At this point you need to ask if you are really living out your focus or if you need to make some profound changes.

It helps to define the leader's role

I soon learnt the key role of the leader is to be the guardian of the church's vision. That guardianship meant being proactive and not assuming everyone was united around the vision. When we started we had been very focused and I naively believed that this would simply continue indefinitely. Everyone knew what the church was about and we had worked on the vision statement together and we all knew it. We started with an excitement about connecting with unchurched people in Huddersfield and I thought we were set fair for the foreseeable future but, as I mentioned earlier, this was not the case.

As I reflected on the events which caused our first crisis, I learnt two important lessons. Firstly, people don't always hear what you think you have said. My words about creating new church were heard in the light of what this might mean for those already in church. Secondly, you cannot afford to assume that people in the church are always on board with the focus and vision of the church. I had assumed we were all together in this because we had started together. But things then developed in different directions. My naïve assumption nearly led to our disintegration.

After this I started to apply the Nehemiah Principle, which simply states that a vision must be restated every 26 days if it is not to be lost.[10] I discovered the truth of that principle the hard way. After this incident, I started to communicate our vision statement to the church as regularly as I could. I created a number of times in the church's calendar to do this. This would usually be on the first Sunday in January, at the church AGM in April, in September when everyone was back from summer holidays and at our church birthday in October. I would effectively do the same talk but dress it up slightly differently on each occasion. No one ever seemed to realise this. I would be simply saying to them, 'Don't forget why we are here. Our vision statement reminds us of this and why we started this adventure together. God has asked us to fulfil this calling and so together today we recommit ourselves to our vision of the future.' I often used people's own stories, especially people who had come to faith recently, to underline the points I had made.

My main role at the Net was keeping our vision alive and constantly in front of us. It meant sometimes I could be a pain as I pointed out yet again what we were there for. But it is important that the 'Why' precedes the 'How' and is always the main driver in the life of the church. The senior leader's role is vital in keeping the main thing the main thing. It's not always easy to do but those first few months showed me the cost to myself and the church if I didn't.

It needs to be the focus throughout all church activities

It is important that the vision of the church is clearly seen in all its activities and not just some. For us, this meant making sure those responsible for all our activities were working out how their groups lived out the vision statement. This was true for our youth and children's activities, for our small groups, for social action and for any other activity. Whenever I met with group leaders, I emphasised to them their unique roles in enabling their group to live out the vision statement in particular ways.

I would use the vision statement even when talking about putting the chairs out. To be honest putting out the chairs at church has to be the worst job! It can seem so mundane and repetitive and it's hard work. But what if you saw that seemingly menial role in the light of our church's vision? What if the chair you put out is sat on by

Colin's story

I joined the Net, with my family, about a year after it had started. I had been at the launch of the church for the local radio station I worked for then. You could say I ended up on the Leadership Team because Dave asked me to join it, but really after being at the church for a couple of years, I wanted to be part of its shaping. The work I do in radio is based on reaching those outside the church and I wanted to use the skills God has given me to help the Net in its aim to reach the person on the street.

To me, the role of the Leadership Team was to support Dave as leader, and to be a sounding board for him. But also it was to steer the vision of the church and ensure that everything we did was filtered through that vision. In my experience, many churches do not set a vision first and so they go off on all sorts of tangents and waste time and resources.

The biggest pressures on the Leadership Team were people and relationships. One of the key values of the church was authentic relationships, so when they went wrong, as they will, it was very painful. We spent lots of meetings creating a conflict resolution document and as soon as we had finished it, we needed to put it into practice. At least this gave us some kind of road map for what we were doing, although it was still very difficult.

Creativity was the second biggest pressure: remaining fresh. It was important to reflect God's creativity: creative ways of connecting with people outside church and creative ways for our worship. For me, the key was surprising people, so they didn't quite know what they were going to get.

When Dave told me he was leaving, I was shocked. He was the Net; it was hard to imagine it without him. We had to pray lots and map out what needed to be done. It meant lots of people getting involved in new ways and doing things they would never have imagined doing. It was an important time in the life of the Net, a real learning time. Now we had to take the church forward.

Working with a new leader was helped by the fact that he knew Dave and he knew the vision of the church. This made it much easier for him to settle in. He also took his time to meet people and to get to know them and to develop relationships. Leadership meetings were led very differently from the way they had been, but that was fine and we still got things done.

someone who then decides to become a follower of Jesus? What if the way the room is set out makes an impact on someone who comes to church for the first time ever? What if you pray over each seat as you put it out, praying for the person who might sit there? You begin to see that even the ways the chairs are put out can make a real difference, not simply for that meeting but for eternity.

There is a danger in all this. I sometimes see churches spending terrific energy on developing their focus or vision statement. They spend hours researching, listening and debating before producing a wonderful vision document. But then the process grinds to a halt. It is never referred to again but put away onto a dusty shelf. Don't put all your energies into creating a vision, because you will need most of your energy to maintain and develop that vision.

It helps to determine the processes

Vision tells you where you want to be. We knew we wanted to be a church that was connecting with unchurched people and was learning to love God and each other more. So our vision then helped us to ask the question of what we needed to put into place to get there. What were the processes that we had to have to ensure that the vision statement was achievable? This is often a step that churches miss out. They produce a vision statement, then fail to ask the supplementary questions about how, step by step, they will achieve the big picture.

For us at the Net this had to start with our relationship with God and the ways we were nurturing it individually and corporately. It was important that we were enabling people to be hungrier for God. I was aware that in the short time people are at church activities, we cannot provide every spiritual nutrient for them, but we can create the environment which enables them to feed themselves.

We were also committed to developing our sense of community and our love and care for each other. One way we did this was to develop more social activities simply so we could spend good time together. On four Sundays a year, we used to go off and do a communal activity together with no formal service part. For many people, these were important moments for developing relationships with others in the church.

It also made us think about how we related to those outside the church. It made us realise the priority we needed to give our friends, workmates, family and social groupings. The danger was that this new church could have sucked people into the maintenance of church activities. We worked hard at trying to ensure people had as much time as possible to develop and nurture their relationships. This is one of the main reasons we tried to limit our church meetings. For this, we developed a mantra that summed up our attitude, 'Minimise meetings and maximise relationships.'

When I talk to leaders who are having problems with their new churches, I would estimate three quarters of the issues revolve around lack of or an unclear vision. Sometimes it has not been clarified clearly or different people are working to competing visions. These things suck energy from the church and divert it from its proper God-given course. I really believe creating and developing a vision has been vital to the Net and was the most significant element in our growth. Without it, I do not believe the Net would be in existence today.

Questions for discussion and reflection

1. What is your vision for the church? How have you defined it?

2. What values are you operating with? Are these implicit or explicit?

3. Are there other visions and values operating within the church?

4. How and where are you communicating the vision and values?

5. How are you measuring your progress as a church?

Books

J. Dunn, *The Effective Leader* (Eastbourne: Kingsway, 1995)

T.S. Rainer and E. Geiger, *Simple Church: Returning to God's process for making disciples* (Nashville: B and H, 2006)

W.C. Wright, *Relational Leadership: A biblical model for influence and service* (Carlisle: Paternoster, 2000)

Essential Four

Mission

Mission is the heartbeat of God

This chapter will be different from others as it will concentrate more on theology than on practice. You may be thinking of turning on to the next chapter now but I would urge you to keep going because without this theology, the rest of how to do it doesn't really make sense.

Don't start with church: start with God

This might seem a strange statement in a book about creating church. Many books plunge straight into what the church needs to be like or do to connect with people in the twenty first century. That is important and this book will help you do that. But the theology of mission in the last sixty years has importantly moved us away from the church as our starting place. Our starting place is not what we do or should do.

We need to go back to God the Trinity as our starting point. The Trinity reminds us that God himself is community as Father, Son and Holy Spirit. God in himself is relational and communal. But this divine community is not a self-serving or inward-looking community. It is a missionary community through which the Father sends the Son into the world through the power of the Holy Spirit. (The word mission literally means sent.) God himself is community in mission and he calls his church to be that same kind of community, a community of love which is always looking and moving outwards. We are not to keep the good news of Jesus wrapped up in our church buildings but, as God's people, we are sent into God's world.[11] Mission emanates from the inner loving community of the Godhead. This is most clearly seen in Jesus' words to the disciples at one of his appearances after the resurrection. He says to them, 'Peace be with you! As the Father has sent me, I am sending you' (Jn. 20:21). Our mission echoes the mission of Jesus. We are a sent people as a consequence of the sending of Jesus by the Father.

I find this a fantastically encouraging place to start as it reminds me that mission is not ultimately my thing or the church's but God's. It means that mission is so much more than one of the tasks of the church or a call to be mission-flavoured. It exists at the very heart of God and he invites us to work with him in his project. It takes away the pressure of seeing this as my work or believing that it all depends on me. What a God we worship, who invites us to be part of Mission Earth.

Before we go any further, it is worth noting that Essential Five will look at evangelism and these two terms, mission and evangelism, are often used inter-changeably. But they do mean slightly different things. Mission tends to have a larger focus and encompasses all of God's work of reconciling the whole of creation to himself. Stuart Murray helpfully reminds us of the immensity of God's mission plans when he writes, 'God's missionary purposes are cosmic in scope, concerned with the restoration of all things, the establishment of shalom, the renewal of creation and the coming of the Kingdom as well as the redemption of fallen humanity and the building of the church.'[12] Evangelism, while being a massive part of God's mission, tends to have a particular focus on the proclamation of the good news of Jesus to enable people to become his disciples.

Don't start with church: start with mission

This might sound like a chicken and egg problem. But actually it is vital and is often the hardest concept for us to grasp. John Finney sums up its importance when he writes, 'Start with the church and the mission will probably get lost. Start with the mission and it's likely that the church will be found.'[13] The danger is that we start with our default positions of church and do mission from there. We start with a fixed outward form of local church and simply invite people to join us in it. This worked to some extent when our society shared our default position but they no longer do. To them the church is alien, as alien as going into a betting shop would be for me. They don't want to come to church as we have so often done it. It is not necessarily the message that creates the barrier but the culture of the church. The mission is planting the seeds of the gospel and beginning to see churches sprouting forth but these need to be churches that take on a shape with regard to their local context. Our task, as we have already seen, is not to produce a type of 'flat pack' church that only requires us to follow a plan and put together the varying parts, as we have always done and always will.

Don't start with church: think about the incarnation

The incarnation, Jesus coming into our world as a human, gives us a wonderful model for our mission. Presumably it would have been much easier for Jesus to remain in heaven and not become human and enter our world. Heaven for Jesus was a safe environment but he stepped out of his comfort zone. God's call of mission upon us as individuals and churches is the same. We are called by God to leave the comfort zone of our church life where we feel safe and secure, and to enter his world outside the walls of our buildings.

The incarnation also helps us to think about how we relate to culture. New churches are often accused of wanting to be relevant at any cost even if it means selling out to the prevailing cultures. The coming of Jesus reminds us that his salvation had a universal range (as it is available to all peoples) but to win this for us, Jesus had to become part of a particular culture. He came in a culturally clothed body: there is no other way to be human. He was born a Jew, into a land occupied by the Roman Empire at the beginning of the first millennium. We are called to embody Christ in a local culture as his body of people. We have to start with the incarnation. Jesus had to become like us before he could die for us. We have to enter into our local culture before we can be counter-cultural, or there is no place for conversation. The church has often had a tendency to want to be counter-cultural first before getting alongside people. We have a tendency, as churches, to tell people immediately what they are doing wrong and how terrible society is. But the danger of this is that it feels to them as if the church is simply condemning them without ever really knowing them. Don't get me wrong here: I am not saying we should not be standing up for God's values but we need to build relationships before this can be effective.

We do need as churches to be aware of becoming so relevant that we lose the uniqueness of our calling. We need to be involved but distinctive. This is a hard balance to maintain. We proclaim an unchanging message but the way we proclaim it has always changed throughout history.

Jesus coming into our world involved both continuity and change: continuity in that he was never less than the Son of God but change as he took on our humanity. In the same way, we are called to create church which has continuity with the past but which is open to change. It is important to stress that we are not being called to reinvent church. In one sense we do not start with a blank sheet. There are certain biblical givens that create church which are unchanging. But the way we live these out has changed throughout history and this is a continuing pattern. The early church in Jerusalem and a modern church today in London would both be church but would look, sound and feel very different from each other. The Church of England and Methodist Church are now using the term 'fresh expressions of church'. I like this term as it does not suggest something totally new but it reminds us that in every generation we need to express freshly what it means to be church. (More about church in Essential Seven.)

Our role as churches is therefore to be constantly discerning how we receive the unchanging gospel in our changing local context. This is what it means to be local missionaries. This is exactly what our fellow Christians do as they are sent to other lands and cultures overseas. We need to wake up to the fact that we are now in that same missionary culture. We have tribes today that need to be reached with the gospel. They are the tribes of football supporters, Goths, the housebound, skaters, sarok dancers, bikers, model car enthusiasts, Internet junkies: the list could go on and on. It is unlikely all these tribes will turn up at a church service so how do we, as the church, connect with them where they are? How does God want us to be sent to them? This is why we started relationship groups in a local gym or worked with the local council in providing presents and a party at Christmas for the children of asylum seekers who had ended up in Huddersfield.

Much of this missionary thinking is summed up in these famous words of Vincent Donovan, an American missionary to the Masai tribe in Tanzania, as he reflected on God's mission back in the West: 'Do not try to call them back to where they were, and do not try to call them to where you are, beautiful as that place may seem to you. You must have the courage to go with them to a place that neither you nor they have been before.'[14] It is scary, as the gospel not only means change for them but also for us. We cannot be involved in God's mission and remain unchanged ourselves. This challenges us to ask which of our cherished practices are we prepared to forfeit for the sake of the gospel.

But we also need to remember that this is not a new phenomenon. It stretches right back to the Apostle Paul. In our day we use the phrase 'all things to all people' as a derogatory term. We often apply it to politicians whom we accuse of saying and doing anything to win our votes. But for Paul, it was a badge of honour. He writes to the church in Corinth, 'Though I am free and belong to no man, I make myself a slave to everyone, to win as many as possible.' He then goes on to say how he has become like various peoples, including Jews and Gentiles, so that they might be able to hear the gospel. He sums up his outlook when he writes, 'I have become all things to all

people so that by all possible means I might save some. I
do all this for the sake of the gospel that I may share in its
blessings' (1 Cor. 9:22–23). The challenge is whether we
are willing to do the same. It is messy and difficult. It
makes us ask questions about what we can and cannot
change. But it is all about being sent by God into the
world that he loves. We cannot start with a preferred
model of church which we can import into any situation.
There is a framework that we operate within but after
that, all sorts of patterns and models are possible to
enable as many people as possible to hear the gospel and
respond to it.

Don't necessarily start church with public worship

A church service is not always the best launch pad for
mission. The pattern for the last few hundred years has
been to start something new with a church service. But
with people with no or little experience of church, maybe
this is no longer the best place to start.

When we started the Net, our first question was not
what kind of service was required. What was paramount
to us was what kind of mission would connect with all
the unchurched people in Huddersfield. We didn't start
public worship services for the first nine months of
getting together. As we then began to develop our
corporate worship we continually asked, how does this
enable unchurched people to encounter the living God?

The Net is only one way of approaching church. We
started with a small community of like minded people
who wanted to connect with unchurched people in
Huddersfield. But this is not the only way to work and
often the starting place, experience is showing us, is in
developing community as the first steps in mission.

Reverend Barbara Glasson, a Methodist minister, came to Liverpool to discover no church and no congregation. She wandered the streets of Liverpool and listened to people. She didn't then start a service but began to gather people together to bake bread; often people who were marginalised. But through people coming together to make bread community was formed, which is now called Somewhere Else. Part of the process of cooking is of course time to chat and share stories. From this, the group started to develop natural ways to talk about Jesus and eventually a simple service began to start.[15]

On the Hartcliffe Estate in Bristol, an area of multiple deprivations, two women and a new curate started praying for their locality. Other people from around the area began to join them to pray. They prayed about how they might reach out to the unchurched people on the estate. What emerged was The Lighthouse. It might not look like a conventional church. It now meets every Friday evening in a house. They come together for a meal. Through this they are forming community, sharing not only a meal together but their lives. There is plenty of space to talk and to share what is happening and to try and discover how Jesus fits into all of it. This seemed to be a much better way forward for this area than starting with a worship service. Since January 2006, they have begun a monthly service in a local community centre.

These are wonderful stories of what God is doing through his people but it is worth noticing that they didn't start with a church service but with developing community which led to evangelism and discipleship and finally a worship service has begun to evolve. My experience is that more and more new churches are finding this to be the way God is leading them.

John's story

In April 2000, I found myself homeless and living rough on the edge of Huddersfield. My home was under a bridge on the canal. I had been living rough on and off for the previous twenty years. Whilst doing this I met a few people who regularly walked past my bridge. They tried to help me out. Some of these people came from the Net church. From advice given me by one couple at the church I was able to get a permanent place to live in Huddersfield. On moving into my new home, the only possessions I owned were carried on my back. On the day I moved in, I went out to the shops and on my return found these few possessions had been stolen. I now had nothing. But the Net and friends of Net members helped me with the basic things I needed.

Shortly after moving in, I was invited to the Net services and was welcomed by a few good people. Not being a Christian, I was invited to a group to find out more about Jesus and the Christian faith. In all honesty I enjoyed the group but it didn't make me feel any different. Then I started meeting with a church small group and I began to get to know people and I started to build relationships with Christians who accepted me for who I was.

On 8th February 2001, I was out shopping when I heard a whisper. 'You need help.' Later on at the bus stop I heard a voice again saying, 'You need help.' I was sure it was God. About an hour later, when I got home I rang one of the people in my small group and told them what had happened and that I wanted to commit my life to Jesus. I knew I wanted my life to change forever.

Don't end with church but continue with mission

It is important that we realise the creation of church is not the final conclusion but is part of the mission dynamic. This dynamic involves:

Connecting: this is the sending dynamic of making contact with those outside the church primarily through relationships.

Community: through these relationships community begins to be formed around Jesus as evangelism and discipleship take place.

Church: this community evolves into something that we might call church.

Commission: we are then called to go out again from this new church as groups of people or teams are sent out to continue the mission dynamic through then making new connections and restarting the process.

There isn't one model of church or community as we live the gospel of Jesus together. It is vital to hear from God and to listen to and understand the community which God is calling you. Please don't simply copy someone else's attempts or hope that there is a failure-free blueprint waiting for you. Realise the heart of God for his world and the principles of God's mission but then discern what kind of community God is calling you to develop in your locality. We could call this 'missional intelligence'. You may not start where you thought you might and you certainly will proceed in directions you never dreamt of but you will be part of God's missional adventure.

Questions for discussion and reflection

1. How do you understand the mission of God?

2. How have you tried to put mission before the church?

3. What are some of the challenges for you in trying to connect with your local cultures? How are you attempting to be incarnational?

Books

Alan Hirsch, *The Forgotten Ways* (Grand Rapids: Brazos Press, 2006)

Andrew Kirk, *What is Mission? Some theological explorations* (London: DLT, 1999)

Michael Moynagh, *Emergingchurch.Intro* (Crowborough: Monarch 2004)

Lesslie Newbigin, *The Open Secret: Introduction to the Theology of Mission* (London: SPCK, 1995)

Christopher Wright, *The Mission of God* (Leicester: IVP, 2006)

Essential Five

Evangelism

Reaching out effectively

As I mentioned earlier what inspired me most to begin the Net was reading some statistics which revealed that 53 per cent of people in Huddersfield had no contact with any religious institution. It forced me to think about the thousands of people of all ages in my town who had no opportunity to hear about Jesus. My passion was to create a church that might connect with them and enable them to hear the good news about Jesus.

I believe that such a passion needs to be at the heart of any plans to create a new church. I talked to a minister who was hoping to start a new church. We were talking about his plans and the team he hopes to take with him. He commented to me that when he talked to the team about evangelism, 'they were like rabbits caught in car headlights.' They were much more interested in what small groups there would be for them and provision for children. This is not unusual as I go around many churches. Often we Christians are more interested in our own comfort than the simple fact that the majority of people in our country are lost for eternity. The danger is that what we receive from following Christ becomes our focus, rather than being witnesses to him and his benefits. What would we make of missionaries we sent overseas if all they asked about was their needs and requirements? We have to wake up to the fact we are missionaries to our own country and must be willing to take the risks and make the sacrifices to enable people to hear and respond to the good news about Jesus. When we concentrate on our needs and are blind to the lostness of those without Christ, the church is in a precarious position.

I would be the first to agree that evangelism is not easy. I was leading a workshop this weekend at a church and one of the participants spoke for many people when he said, 'I know I should be doing evangelism, but I just don't want to and I feel guilty about that.' I admired his honesty.

I see a loss of confidence in evangelism even among the liveliest churches, combined with a feeling that evangelism doesn't work in today's world. Certainly it takes people much longer now to decide to become disciples of Jesus. This process of coming to faith may take a few years of getting to know a Christian friend, coming to a few services, attending a nurture course like Alpha, reading some books and so on. With much less background knowledge of Christianity, few people are ready to make an instant decision and so the impression is given that it doesn't happen like it used to.

Evangelism has also had a bad press through the tele-evangelists of America. We have rightly reacted against slick presentations and dubious morals but bad models do not make evangelism wrong. Nor is our cultural climate conducive to evangelism. Our world triumphs that all views are equally valid and we should not suggest we have any answers that might be better than anyone else's.

Last summer, I was in America meeting lots of church leaders throughout the country. Very few of them wanted to talk about evangelism and some of them were hostile to the subject because of the negative stereotypes they associated with the word. They felt more relaxed using terms like missional but they did not want to associate with anything that was related to evangelism. We may need to rethink evangelism for today's world but we must not let that stop us putting it as our priority in starting new churches. We do not want to create something that is simply more entertaining, more relevant or funkier: we need churches that create an environment for unchurched people to meet with Jesus. If we don't do that, we have failed in our main task.

I think it is important that we define what we mean by evangelism so that we are clear exactly what we are talking about. I like the missiologist David Bosch's definition. He writes, 'evangelism is the core, heart or centre of mission; it consists in the proclamation of salvation in Christ to non-believers in announcing forgiveness of sins, in calling people to repentance and faith in Christ, inviting them to become living members of Christ's earthly community and to begin a life in the power of the Holy Spirit.'[16] Surely such a definition must be at the heart of our work of creating new church.

The following experience which happened to one of my good friends from Huddersfield when she visited her local church underlines the need to have evangelism at the centre of our church life. She was seeking spiritual answers to her life. She would come to our house and before I could even say 'Hello' she would be asking us about why we thought God would allow people to suffer. One Sunday morning, she woke up and felt God clearly saying to her, 'Go to church this morning.' Not surprisingly, this blew her mind. But she felt it was so clearly God speaking that she decided she had better do what God said and go to church. The Net did not have a service that morning, so she decided to go to her local church's morning service.

As she arrived at the church, she was feeling so nervous. On entering the church building, she was greeted with these words, 'What are you doing here?' This is not the classic greeting to be given to a newcomer. My friend said the underlying assumption of the question was that nobody would actually choose to spend an hour of their lives in that place, so what on earth what she doing there? She decided it might be too much to answer, 'God told me to come here,' and so she mumbled something about coming to have a look at the church.

Then she went to find somewhere to sit. She sat near the front and discovered she had sat right in the middle of a baptism party. She couldn't get out of that church quick enough at the end. After the service she understood why she had been asked that question about why she was there. As an outsider, she said to me, 'I felt like I had stumbled into a secret club. Nothing was explained, the assumption was that you knew what to do, when to stand and what to read and it all seemed so irrelevant to my life. There was no hint of expectation that anyone from outside the church might come in and so everything that was done was geared for those who were there week after week.' Not surprisingly, she did not rush back.

At the Net, we wanted to create a place where connecting with unchurched people was central to everything we did; where the assumption was that people from outside the church would be at everything we did; where we thought about their comfort and the issues they were facing and created a safe environment to hear about Jesus.

We found, right from day one, that we *were* attracting people who never normally came to church. Originally we had thought we would have special events for them and that our worship services would be for Christians. But soon we found that unchurched people were coming to our services as well. It was strange that at the same time that some of the original team were struggling with what we were doing others were finding faith, sometimes in the most dramatic way.

Angela is a lively person, a mother of three who lectures in a FE college in Huddersfield. She lived next door to some people from the Net who invited her to our first carol service. After that she came to a number of church events, some purely social, others with more Christian content. She really enjoyed the events with their multi-media clips and casual approach and starting coming to our Sunday event with her husband and three children. She also started coming to a small group we ran for people to explore the Christian faith. We called it 'Just Looking' simply because it is for people who want to have a quick look at the Christian faith. Following the six weeks of this course, she was very close to becoming a Christian.

One week we had a guest speaker who said at the end of his talk, 'If you want to follow Jesus, would you please stand up.' This was not something we usually did at the Net. There was silence and nobody moved. It would have been easy to think that the evening had been a failure. But nobody knew the impact it had on Angela. In her own indomitable words she said later, 'My bum cheeks were an inch away from getting off the seat.' But her bum was not to stay seated for long.

The next week we had a normal Sunday gathering. Strangely I remember saying to Heather that my talk was particularly aimed at those who had been Christians for some time, to challenge them about not becoming complacent. Little did I know how God was at work. At the end of my talk, I heard some movement in the chairs in the third row right in front of me. I looked up and could see Angela was getting to her feet. She said, 'Dave, could I say a few words?' In the next five seconds a hundred questions whizzed through my mind. What heresy might she say? What had I said that might have offended her? What do I do now? One of the great things about working with people who are not used to being in church is that they don't realise that you are not meant to suddenly stand up and call a halt to the proceedings. I nervously replied, 'Go on then, Angela.' To all our astonishment she said, 'I want to tell you all that I want to become a follower of Jesus, I am ready to become one of his disciples. Last week I couldn't stand up when the speaker asked us to, so I'm standing up now.' There was silence as we took in what she was saying. She was in tears and as I realised what she was saying I felt tears rolling down my cheeks as well. Most of the people present were in tears. Later she said to me about that moment, 'It was as though God had reached down into my heart and touched it.' It was an amazing few minutes. But it did not stop there.

Somehow we managed to get through the rest of the service. But then a ripple effect began. After the service had ended, two other people who had been in the Just Looking group with Angela came to Heather and me and said. 'We want to become disciples of Jesus too. We weren't as brave as Angela but we want to do the same thing.' We prayed with them. Later we discovered another person had gone home and decided to follow Jesus. She made the same decision on her own and told us the next week. There was a vicar visiting us from Bradford that day who said to me as we were packing up,

'This must have been what the early church in Acts was like.' Now I hasten to add that our gatherings were not usually like this. As I walked back to the car after the meeting, a taxi driver opened his window and stopped me. I thought to myself, surely he's not going to ask me how to become a Christian. He didn't, just the directions to a certain road!

The memories and emotions of that Sunday morning will live with me for ever. Angela's bum cheeks will always remind me that evangelism is central to all that we are and do as churches!

The very first words of Mark's gospel are, 'The beginning of the gospel about Jesus Christ, the Son of God' (Mk. 1:1). The Greek word for gospel is the word from which we derive our word evangelism. For non-Jews reading these verses, the word gospel was an incredibly positive term: to them it meant party. It was the term used to describe the celebration of the Roman Emperor's birthday. I wonder how many of us would describe evangelism as party time? I suspect that this is the total opposite of many of our feelings about evangelism.

When we started the Net, we were convinced that Huddersfield did not need just another church. There were too many churches already in the town and some had already closed. But it did need more churches that were seeking to connect with unchurched people, whose aim was to make a priority of the majority of the town who had no contact with any church. We cannot simply reproduce church models that suit us, with little regard to the needs of those outside the church. The welcome of my friend was a scandal which does not reflect anything about the nature of God himself or his church. But I suspect that her experience of church was not an unfortunate exception. Is it not better for us to take some risks for God than to preserve the status quo in the safety and seclusion of a 'safe-lived' life? We need more churches that are willing to put the party time of the good news about Jesus at the centre of all they do. If we don't, is there really any point in creating something new? Why would we want to create even more churches for people that already go to church?

So why would we do this thing we call evangelism or why should our church?

It reflects the nature of Jesus

'For the Son of Man came to seek and save what was lost' (Lk. 19:10). This phrase, used at the end of Jesus' meeting with Zacchaeus, sums up so much about his priorities. The religious people's complaint was that 'He has gone to be the guest of a sinner.' They were thinking that if Jesus knew anything, he should be concentrating on them. Surely they were the ones who were more favoured by God. Yet at whose house did Jesus stay for the night? It wasn't with the local religious leaders but with the notorious tax collector Zacchaeus.

The key was the way Jesus saw people. He didn't see them as the religious leaders did. They viewed people as in or out with God and believed God was only interested in the insiders. But Jesus saw people as God the Father saw them: individuals that he loved and longed for and hoped would respond to that love. Jesus makes it clear that God has a tender heart towards those who do not know him yet. Our calling is to see people in that same way. Luke 15 probably sums this up best. Again, the setting for this is the grumbling of the religious leaders about those Jesus was spending time with. Yet as Jesus tells the stories of the lost sheep, coin and son, he makes clear God's priority to those outside the church. It is disastrous to leave ninety-nine sheep alone while looking for just one lost sheep, but this sums up the crazy love of God. Above all, the tale of the lost son gives us an amazing picture of a father constantly looking to see if his son might be returning. This is our God, who always wants to welcome those on the outside into his presence and his community.

We need to ask ourselves whether our hearts are becoming like God's. The danger is always that we get so caught up in running church that we forget what it's for. We begin to believe that the church exists solely for those who are already part of it, when our priority must be towards those who have yet to connect with the good news about Jesus.

It reflects our relationship with God

At its most simple, evangelism is the authentic overflow of our daily encounters with the risen Jesus. It is not something extra to our normal Christian life. Or to go back to Mark's gospel, it must be party for us before it can be party for anyone else.

We tend to talk about whatever we are excited about. It's very normal. Listen to any conversation in a playground, pub or staff room and you will discover that. We are much more likely to express something about God if we are experiencing him in our lives. If at the moment you feel God is distant, a burden or a killjoy, or if he engenders feelings of guilt in you, why would you want to inflict him on anyone else? For anyone involved in church leadership, at any level, the biggest danger is the work done for God can have the potential to destroy the work of God in us. Running groups, leading meetings, coping with the pressing pastoral issues or the ever-growing administration can take us away from God's amazing love for us.

In all this the most destructive element is our busyness. It is so easy to lose our heart for God and for his mission in the middle of all we have to do. The whirlpool of church activity can suck the spiritual life from us. It is so easy even for a new church to spend all its energies keeping the thing going and so quickly lose sight of why it was created.

So how do we create and develop a church that has and keeps evangelism at its very heart? Even in new churches, I keep talking to leaders who say that the number of people coming to faith is small because they have lost a sense of what their mission is. I believe we do need to be strategic in this as a church. It does not just happen and there always seems to be evangelism slippage as this priority melts away. I believe there are four important keys that can help with this.

Envision

This takes us back to the importance of focus. Someone needs to be reminding the church of what evangelism might look like in your situation. This is where I found our vision statement so helpful in continually reminding us why we were doing what we were doing.

We need to help people in churches to be passionate and confident about the good news of Jesus and to want to share it with those around them at home, at work, in their community or their social lives. They are the key people, if evangelism is to happen in the local church. There is no one else; they are God's people for that place.

We need to find ways to help people to see God can use them as they are, not as they think they should be. One of the biggest dangers is people's preconceived ideas of what someone involved in evangelism is like. Either they don't want to be like that or they don't feel they could be like that, even if they wanted to be. But if evangelism is simply that authentic overflow of our relationship with Jesus then we can all be involved in small but significant ways.

In a previous church, whenever I asked people how they had joined the church, one name would invariably crop up: Mary Moorhouse. Not that Mary was your archetypal evangelist. She was a quiet, shy seventy-year-old woman and the secret of her evangelistic success was not something you would hear about in a training programme. She went round selling copies of the church magazine! But as she did this, she would talk to anybody and quickly formed relationships and invited people to church. I once asked her about her strategy. She denied she had one or that she was any good at evangelism. But she certainly was. She had the basic requirements for evangelism. She loved God and she loved people.

The wonderful truth is that God uses us as we are, even in our brokenness. We don't have to wait till we attain a particular spiritual level before we can be involved in evangelism. Evangelism is about grace. God wants to use us as we are, where we are, for his work of evangelism.

I found the best way to envision people was to get them to concentrate on God and those outside the church. It is important to keep emphasising that, ultimately, this is God's work. This takes much of the pressure away from us and reminds us of the importance of prayer and our own spiritual life, rather than evangelistic techniques. The evangelist Rebecca Manley Pippert writes

At one conference a woman raised her hand and said 'If evangelism is essentially a spiritual activity that is

predicated on the supernatural power of God, then how do I
tap into the Spirit's power? What is the role of prayer and
fasting in evangelism?' ... What stunned me about her
comment was that it was the first time anyone had ever
raised this issue in all the years I've done training.[17]

Where are we finding time and space as a church to pray
about and for mission? In Huddersfield, the most natural
place to do this was through the small groups. We also
did simple things like producing book marks on which
people could write the names of friends, for whom they
could pray regularly.

Encourage

It's not enough only to envision people about evangelism. How do we encourage them to get involved in it?
    I think there are two simple ways to do this. The first is
to explain what their role in the evangelism strategy is.
We need to take the pressure off people, especially those
who find evangelism frightening. At the Net, we did not
expect everyone to be able to explain the gospel to their
friends, answer all their questions and then lead them
into a relationship with Jesus. I think this scenario
petrifies people. We had some people who could do this
but it was not the norm.

There were three things we expected people to be able to
do: firstly, to pray regularly for a few specific people;
secondly, to tell the story of how they came to faith and
the difference Jesus was currently making to their lives;
and thirdly, to invite others to social and evangelistic
events we held at the Net. We saw our strategy as
cooperation between church members and what we did
centrally. We had to make sure that the events we put on

were of such a quality that people were confident to bring their friends to them, knowing that they would not be cringeworthy.

Initially, we had an evangelistic event every month, but we found this hard to maintain because of the time required to organise and put these events on. So then we organised them bimonthly. As I said earlier, these events were never on a Sunday morning, as we found that was not a good time for unchurched people. Friday or Saturday evening were much better times. These events were totally focused on those invited from outside the church. We tried to hire pleasant venues, often with food and a bar, to help people feel comfortable. We tried lots of events, from multi-media presentations around a theme such as stress or what would Jesus say to David Beckham? We had evenings where people were interviewed, including professional Christian sportspeople or those who had been involved in national tragedies. For example we interviewed a father whose daughter died in the Lockerbie air crash. We often found these interviews worked better than a straight talk, as people loved to discover the details of other people's lives. We wanted to give church people the confidence to bring their friends because of the quality of the presentation. I remember once we had an amazing Christian magician/comedian called John Archer. John is wonderfully talented and funny and has a powerful testimony. When he came about sixty people attended but he was so good we invited him back a year later and we sold out of our one hundred and twenty tickets a long time before the event. Having heard him once, people were even more confident to bring their friends along.

At the end of any event, we had cards for people to fill in on which they could make comments about the evening but also through which they could sign up for our nurture course. Our aim for these meetings was to see some people sign up for the course.

We also had lots of social events to which people could bring friends who might not be ready for something with more Christian content. These included everything from meals to ten pin bowling, or days out at farm parks. The advantage of these was that when these people then came along to our evangelistic events, they already knew some of the people in the church.

Our strategy was simple. It involved individual relationships leading to church events and the possibility of then attending a nurture course. Individuals needed to tell their stories to those around them and to invite people to events. We always made sure we gave people lots of time to pray and invite people to our events. Our corporate role was to put on excellent events and to provide follow-up for those interested, that enabled them to find out more about Jesus and to respond to him. This simple strategy worked really well. I found the people in the Net the best inviters I have ever come across. It was rare for less than 50 per cent of the total attendance to be made up of invited guests at any of our events. I know from speaking at events at other churches that this is unusual.

Many recent books about church can be negative about invitational events. They suggest that such attractional events, where you are inviting people to church events, should now be replaced by what is called more incarnational church; that is where the church is working out how to be Christian out in the world without expecting people to come to us. Eddie Gibbs notes in his book on emerging church that

the direction of church changed from centripetal (flowing in) to a centrifugal (flowing out) dynamic. This in turn led to a shift from attracting crowds to equipping, dispersing and multiplying Christ followers . . . when Christians focus on a 'come structure' for church they cease to be missional in that they are asking those outside the Christian faith to come into their world instead of serving in the world of those outside.[18]

I often hear people saying we need to move from 'coming' to 'going' as the primary movement of the church. As a basic pattern of mission, it reflects God's mission, but it can create an artificial division in terms of church activities. If you look at Jesus' ministry, he both invited people to come to him and he went to where people were. You find the same pattern in the New Testament church: the church in Acts 2 was attractional. Paul's discussion concerning using prophecy and tongues in church (1 Cor. 12:1–25) suggests he expected unchurched people to attend. There are elements of both come to and go to in Jesus' ministry and the New Testament church.

But church needs more than just invitational events, partly because we all have limits to the number of people we can invite to any meeting. We need to be asking how we can connect with people who have no friends who are part of any church. We have tried a number of activities. These included running a relationship seminar for a local gym, running a spiritual discussion group in a town centre coffee shop, gardening makeovers for people whose gardens were badly overgrown, and organising a football coaching course for children and youth. The purpose of all these activities was to get beyond our contact circles and to enable us to connect with as many unchurched people as possible.

An essential for our strategy was proximity. We encouraged people to be near to those outside the church, to step out of their worlds and enter the world of those around them.

One of the original team who was a recent Christian left the Net for another church to be with his fiancée. I spoke to him a few months later and he told me excitedly how he was at church every night of the week for some church activity or social. The danger was that the church had created an alternative social life for him. The saddest element was that as a result he had lost contact with his many non-Christian friends.

Enable and equip

It is important that people feel confident and equipped to tell their story and develop their relationships. We used various evangelistic training courses to give confidence about evangelism and to help people to know how to talk about their faith naturally.[19] It was important that they felt confident in what we were asking them to do.

Example

Finally, it is important that all those involved in leadership at any level take the lead in evangelism and make it clear that they are developing relationships and talking about their faith in their private world. As much as I could, I would talk about conversations I had with people. I often used my talks at church to give examples of this: and not just examples of when it worked but also when I kept quiet or people I invited didn't want to come to a church event. If you are a leader, it's important that you are doing yourself whatever you are asking people to do. That also means you need the time to develop these relationships.

I loved going to my gym in Huddersfield. It was 'my time' away from all the pressures of ministry. I remember once going into the steam room and there was a guy

Jim is 43, married for fourteen years, with two sons. For most of his life, he has worked in sales and marketing, and he came to faith at the Net.

Jim's story

I am a reasonable barometer of your target market. There are a lot of people like me. I was christened as a baby for some reason but between then and the age of 26, I went into a church once. I then met my wife-to-be, who was a Christian. Occasionally I went to church to keep her happy. But it was totally irrelevant to me; I could not see the point of it. I once told some people from my wife's church, 'You have the best story ever and the worst marketing known to mankind.'

The Net took away all my arguments and objections about church. It seemed relevant, real and alive. It dealt with the issues that were important to my life, in a style that worked for me. It had a 'for-me-ness' about it. It started when a number of people from the Net started to invite me to various activities. Then I met Dave at a mutual friend's BBQ. Through that, I was invited to a Just Looking course and my journey really started. Also a close friend died in a motorbike accident, which really got me thinking. I realised my reaction to this tragedy was very different from how I would have reacted previously.

Initially I thought I had to understand everything before I could be a Christian but then I realised it was an ongoing journey with Christ, one that I am now very much on. Some of my questions have been answered but not all of them.

I'm now involved in the planning team for a new congregation at the Net and my grand title is Head of Catering. But I also want to use my 'outside eyes' to develop our plans, as this whole thing is still very fresh to me. I still remember how off-putting church used to be. I want others to discover church as I have found it.

sitting there about my age. He was very chatty and soon asked me about what I did. Usually my answer 'I'm a church leader' thwarted any further conversation. Not this time, though: he stunned me by replying, 'I've been wanting to talk to someone like you. I have a really successful business and I'm making lots of money but it isn't satisfying me. I've been thinking, what is the real point of life? But none of my friends want to talk with me about this.' We had a wonderful conversation about Jesus and the meaning of life. It left me feeling amazed and saddened and made me reflect on two things. Firstly, isn't God's grace wonderful, using me in that situation? I can assure you this wasn't the normal conversation I had in the steam room! I can't even claim that I had prayed as I opened the door. I am convinced, though, that God wants to use us more than we expect, because he loves people so much.

Secondly, I wondered how many other people are there living near us, in our work place or college, in our club or even in our family, who want to talk to someone about the big questions of life? It saddens me that there are thousands of people asking the questions but nobody to help them find the answers. Are we prepared to be the people and churches that are willing to step out of our comfort zones to connect with them?

Questions for discussion and reflection

1. How do you feel about evangelism?

2. Does evangelism have a priority in your church?

3. Do you have a clearly defined strategy for the church, both collectively and for individuals?

4. Is evangelism authentic overflow for you?

Books

John Clarke, *Evangelism that Really Works* (London: SPCK, 1995)

Michael Green, *Evangelism Through the Local Church* (London: Hodder Stoughton, 1990)

Rebecca Manley Pippert, *Out of the Saltshaker* (Leicester: IVP, 1999)

Nick Pollard, *Evangelism Made Slightly Less Difficult* (Leicester: IVP, 2004)

Robert E. Webber, *Ancient-Future Evangelism* (Grand Rapids: Baker, 2003)

Essential Six

Community

The power of community and how to build it

I was interested in evangelism, not community. That would have been my mindset for the majority of my Christian life. I'd leave all this feelings stuff to people with pastoral gifts. My call was to be out there, not worrying about creating community. As far as I was concerned community was for wimps.

How little I knew! Fortunately God dealt with me gently and patiently; I honestly believe that without what I was about to learn, the Net would have failed. The danger would have been that in my missionary zeal I would have continually driven the church people to death while providing little community. I would have created a real divide between evangelism and community. Forgive me if I take some time to tell you the story but it is important.

The need for community

It all started before the Net ever emerged. I was helping to organise a week to help married couples and was looking for some extra resources. A friend told me about some new material that his vicar was using. I rang the vicar and asked him if he could send the materials. Strangely he said he couldn't but could Heather and myself come to a twenty four hour retreat to hear more with other couples in leadership? I only wanted the materials but was persuaded, especially as he said we would be put up in a smart hotel for free.

So off Heather and I went to a hotel in Leicestershire. Being a Christian event, we thought it would be a two star type hotel, if we were lucky! When we pulled into the drive of the hotel, we could not believe what we saw. It was a five star country house hotel, like nothing we had ever stayed in before.

The speakers were an American couple from Texas, David and Teresa Ferguson. Once we got past their thick Texan accents, we discovered two wonderful teachers and vulnerable, caring leaders.

I was hit straight between the eyes when David started talking from Genesis 2:18. 'The Lord God said, "It is not good for the man to be alone. I will maker a helper suitable for him."' It is embarrasing to admit but I had never realised that something was not good in the Garden of Eden before the Fall. How had I missed that? It stands out in stark contrast to the five proceeding goods of Genesis 1 which finish with the resounding, 'God saw all that he had made and it was very good' (Gen. 1:31). Now suddenly there was a *not good* in the perfection of Eden. Remember this is not linked to the Fall and sin, which is not part of the narrative until Genesis 3. As David said, if God says something is not good, then you really are in trouble.

It is worth having a recap on Adam's situation. He lived in the perfect environment with no problems. There was no pollution, no dangers from ecological disasters.

He had the perfect job. He was CEO of Planet Earth for God, responsible for the proper use of the world's resources. Finally he never had problems in his relationship with God. It was perfect. He never struggled to pray or spend time with God. Adam possessed the perfect place to live, the perfect job and the perfect relationship with God. That's what you call living. We would give anything to have those three components in our lives. But suddenly God says it's *not good*. How could that be?

What was missing? Simply, it was other human beings. Although this passage is related to marriage I think it has far wider implications for all relationships. In the next few verses, Adam gives names to the animals but they cannot be his community, he needs someone like him and so woman is formed. As one commentator says, God was not enough and nor were the animals enough: Adam needed other human beings.

The implications of this account from Genesis are huge for our lives and for creating community. For the biblical truth is that we need more than God. You may feel that this sounds like heresy. It seems strange writing it but I can see no other conclusion from the biblical text. We were made by God primarily to need him but also to need other human beings. But often what I hear from church is all you need to do is to sort out your relationship with God, pray more, listen to more sermons or read more Christian books. These may well be part of the answer but they cannot be the whole thing, because it *is not good to be alone*.

We need others to be part of the answer, as they minister God's love, grace, forgiveness and healing to us. Yes, sometimes God deals with us directly, but many other times we experience him through the action of others. Much of this is summed up in Jesus' answer about what is the greatest commandment. This was an age old question for the Jews. Jesus' answer sums up our need for God and each other. We are to love God but also we need to love others. Everything else we do, Jesus says, hangs on this (Mt. 22:34–40).

Not only do we need others, it is *not good for us to be alone*. This doesn't mean solitude is wrong: it means ultimately we were not designed to be 'stand alone' people. One of the best descriptions of aloneness comes from Eimear Montgomerie. In an interview about her marriage to the famous golfer Colin Montgomerie in the *Daily Telegraph*, she said, 'I needed support but Colin wasn't able to give me any. Even when he was back between tournaments he was only there physically, never emotionally.'[20]

How often I meet people who feel isolated and alone even with a busy diary, a hectic schedule and lots of people around them. On the outside, they are successful, well-respected and look as though they have it all together; underneath they are experiencing the pain of aloneness. Their relationships skim the surface and there is nobody who they feel is simply there for them.

This concept of aloneness has been taken further by Robert Putnam.[21] In his book, Putnam identifies the disconnection and aloneness taking place in society which, he claims, is affecting our social structures and massively impacting our physical and civic health. There is a terrible price to pay for our isolation. The writer's views have been sought by many of the governments of the Western world as they grapple with the issues of aloneness.

We also need to understand that this need for others is not a weakness or due to sin. This was all before the Fall. Often I hear people ask, 'What is wrong with me that I need this attention or encouragement? If I was really

mature, I wouldn't need it.' No, this reflects the way God
has made us, we need God but he has also made us to
need each other. We are mutually dependent creatures. In
many ways, we are the sum total of the people we are
connected to and for some of us that thought is
particularly scary.

I wish that I could tell you that hearing this teaching
over twenty-four hours made me go out and change my
life immediately. I certainly enjoyed what I heard and it
made me think. But I am much more stubborn than that.
I remember, as we left the venue, saying to David
Ferguson how much I had enjoyed it but I was an
evangelist: this kind of stuff was good for my wife
Heather though!

Yet graciously over the next few months what I had
heard began to make more and more sense to me and I
began to see that there was no massive divide between
evangelism and community. Community was not for
wimps: it was at the centre of God's plans for his world.
As I read the Bible, I kept seeing how central community
was to God's plan and mission. I realised that the Bible
was not really a book about individual spiritual heroes,
which is often the way it's taught, but about God's
people, his community.

God as community

This is not surprising as God himself, as Trinity, reminds
us that community is at the very core of the Godhead. At
the heart of God is the community of the Father, Son and
Holy Spirit. The communities God asks us to create
reflect his nature.

So how does God communicate his presence to people
in the Old Testament? It is through a community, called

the nation of Israel. In Genesis 12, God calls Abram to move out from the comfort of his surroundings to be the father of a new nation. God says to him, 'I will make you into a great nation and I will bless you; I will make your name great and you will be a blessing. I will bless those who bless you, and whoever curses you I will curse and all peoples on earth will be blessed through you' (Gen. 12:2–3). God's way to bless the whole world was through a community.

The Old Testament also reminds us that God's community is not always perfect. The next stage in God's plan is the coming of Jesus. What does he form around him? Simply, he created a community. He committed himself and his message to this small community of disciples who would continue his work. Some of Jesus' final words to his disciples remind us of the importance of community. Jesus said to them, 'May they be brought to complete unity to let the world know that you sent me and have loved them even as you have loved me' (Jn. 17:23). For Jesus there was a clear link between the community and what that communicated about God and his character. Their life together was evangelistic. Gilbert Bilezikian stresses the importance of community when he writes, 'Jesus knew that if the church should fail to demonstrate community to the world, it would fail to accomplish its mission because the world would have reason to disbelieve the gospel.'[22]

The danger is that we can think of community as an inwardly focused group, only interested in itself while looking to escape from the realities of everyday life. But the community of God's people should always be looking outside itself as it reflects the nature of God himself in the Trinity.

Jesus prays that for us too. 'My prayer is not for them alone. I pray also for those who will believe in me through their message, that all of them may be one, Father, just as you are in me and I am in you. May they also be in us so that the world may believe that you sent me' (Jn. 17:20–21). We are called to be community in mission not community in isolation from God's world. Gilbert Bilezikian comments, 'In our day whenever the church is ineffective and its witness remains unproductive, the first questions that must be raised are whether the church functions as authentic community?'[23]

Then what happens after Jesus' ascension? Acts 2 makes it clear that one of the first actions of the disciples was to create a new community based around the risen Jesus. Most of the rest of the New Testament is not written to individuals but to communities of believers in cities and towns throughout the Roman Empire. Much of the content of the writings is how they are to live out the community life. One scholar has argued that 44 per cent of the New Testament letters are about how to get on with each other. Perhaps the best example is the use over fifty times of the phrase 'one another' to remind Christians to love one another, accept one another, serve one another etc.

And how does the Bible end? It ends spectacularly with community, with the new Jerusalem of Revelation 21, a community where God will reside in a way that is even beyond his presence in Eden. The answer to the aloneness of Adam in Genesis 2 is clearly seen in John's description: 'They will be his people, and God himself will be with them and be their God' (Rev. 21:3). The new community will be with God and with each other.

The Bible is so clear that community is at the heart of God's plans, not an optional extra for people with particular needs. As Bilezikian says, 'God has one priority project throughout history, one that he will bring to climatic completion at the end of history – the formation of new community.'[24] Yet somehow I had missed that. To be fair to myself, I don't ever remember hearing anyone talking about this kind of thing.

I believe God wanted to teach me this before I ever got near starting a new church. He wanted me to understand how he felt about community before I started the long process of creating one. I think without this I would have created some kind of mission station that just concentrated on getting people in but which never went much beyond that. God wanted me to see the association of community and evangelism and to understand that the telling of the gospel was a community event as well as a personal one.

This material also had a profound impact on me personally as it unlocked the pain and hurt I had stored up over a father who had never communicated to me by words or deeds that he loved me. I used to say to Heather that it never bothered me and that I hadn't been affected by this or by him walking out on us when I was fourteen. Yet all that hurt stopped me being able to love others, as I had to submerge all my feelings to keep this hurt at bay. I remember driving in the car with Heather as she spoke to me and God worked in me. I cried and cried. It was as though I was letting the pent-up pain of many years escape so I had more capacity for the positives of life. God was preparing me for what was to come with the Net and increasing my capacity to love his community.

Defining community

Community is certainly sexy at the moment. It seems to be a buzz word of our society as well as the church. It can be linked with almost any word, to create such things as community radio, community development, community engagement, community care, community planning, community justice, community enterprise: the list could almost fill the rest of this book. The problem is that in many books on the subject, there is little attempt to define the term community. It seems to be one of those terms which we think we understand, but whose reality is more complex. Maybe if we can understand more about what community is, we will be more likely to create it on the ground.

For example, there are different types of community.

1. **Geographic community or the community of location.** The location can be very small or it can be national or even global. I think this is the community vicars and pastors talk about when they use phrases like 'my community' or 'the community I serve.'

2. **Communities of culture or communities of need or identity.** These kinds of community often revolve around interest groups, shared hobbies, ethnic groupings etc. These communities can be geographic but are often not, people being drawn together by some other external factor.

3. **Community organisations.** These can be either formal or informal groups including everything from hobbies, social action groups and professional bodies related to work. These organisations would obviously include churches.

Now any church community could be part of any or all of these three groups. The problem is that single English word community can mean many things and we need to be clear about our particular use of it in any given circumstance. So as we talk about creating church community, are we thinking about a geographical identity, a church for a particular place, a group of particular types of people or an official organisation?

I have found Joe Myers' book very helpful in thinking what exactly we mean by community from a Christian perspective.[25] Myers suggests that when we consider community, we immediately think of small groups and offer them as the universal panacea for all community issues in church. But he argues, 'All belonging is significant. Healthy community is achieved when we hold harmonious relationships within all four spaces.'[26] He argues these four spaces are

1. Public space
2. Social space
3. Personal space
4. Intimate space

We need all four. We need community in different ways from the big crowd to time with a very few close friends. A church needs to be creating community when everyone is together, when smaller groups are meeting and when twos and threes join up.

It is also important to ask what makes up our perception of what is good community. Research by two social psychologists, McMilan and Chavis, might help us. They have attempted to define the elements that make up our sense of community. Out of this they have even created a sense of community index to help community groups measure how they are doing.[27]

These are the four factors:

Factor 1: Membership

What does it mean to belong and identify with this group?

As we started the Net for the initial group we were fairly directive concerning what it meant to belong. We needed people to know what their commitment would look like. But working with unchurched people, the sense of belonging was very different. Most people were attracted to us because of relationships with others in the church. They were invited by a friend and liked what they experienced, both through the formal services/ groups but also through the informal relationships and the feel of the place. This was why social occasions were so important for us, to enable people to feel that sense of belonging.

A popular phrase currently in church circles is 'Belonging before believing.' In previous times, people came to faith and then decided to join a church whereas now more people start coming along as part of the community, and within community begin to find a relationship with God. The danger is we can give the impression that unless you become a Christian before the end of this nurture course or within six months or three evangelistic meetings, then you are no longer welcome. We tried to create a community where you could keep on looking and searching for as long as you liked and yet were still as welcome as ever.

After a year or so, I was aware there was a danger of us developing two tiers of belonging. There was the core group of the original members and then the people that joined subsequently. The problem could be the core group would be the first class citizens and the others would somehow be second class. We decided to create some kind of membership system. Initially this was to be based around faith in Jesus. But then I heard someone who had recently started coming to the Net talking to one of my neighbours. In the conversation she referred to me as 'My vicar.' That phrase struck me. They were words of belonging and community. How could we incorporate that into membership, even though presently she was clear she wasn't a believer?

The Leadership Team had long discussions about this. During this process two men who had not yet decided to become disciples of Jesus asked if they could join the church if we were to have a membership system. All my previous experience had told me membership was for those on the inside, the Christians. In the end, we decided that for them, this was their church, and we needed to recognise that. So our membership did not involve an assertion of faith but all that was required was assent that you were in agreement with the mission statement of the church. These people were very happy to do this, as they were very content with the aims of the church, even though presently they were still seeking Jesus. People were happy to identify with a church which explicitly aimed to help unchurched people discover Jesus. This assent was given publicly during a service, usually at our yearly church birthday celebrations. This may seem like a small thing but it was important element in helping us to create a community where people really felt they belonged.

Factor 2: Influence

How could people have influence over what was happening and feel influenced by the group as a whole? I think people feel they belong when they are part of what is going on. That is so much easier when the church is small and everyone is therefore involved with the running of the church. But there are ways people can feel their influence counts. The first is simply being asked what they think. It is important to give people space to be involved in current discussions within the church. This can be done informally through individual conversations, or more formally through questionnaires or group discussions. Firstly, for example, we gave everyone a chance to say what they thought about small groups when we considered changing them. This was done through both a questionnaire and meetings with members of the Leadership Team.

Secondly, it was through being involved in and contributing to the life of the community. There are so many ways to use your skills and it is important for people to feel that they are valued. Anyone and everyone can contribute in some way, if they want, to the group's common life.

Within all of this, I do believe that good communication is vital. People are much more likely to feel they belong if they know what is happening. One of the best things we developed was a weekly email which simply reminded people of something from our worship gathering, and included a joke, news of what was happening that week and future events and dates.

Factor 3: Integration and fulfilment of needs

How are people becoming part of the whole and having their needs met?

Probably my favourite story about Jesus is his encounter with Zacchaeus (Lk. 19:1–10). Jesus met this notorious character, who is hated by most people in the city of Jericho for good reasons. A modern equivalent might be a drugs baron. I am sure that when Jesus called him down from the tree all the people expected him to get the greatest dressing down ever witnessed. He had defrauded half the population and dishonoured his Jewish upbringing; surely this new teacher would let him have it? So there is total shock as Jesus invited himself to stay 'Chez Zacchaeus'. This meant staying overnight. To do such a thing was to totally associate and align yourself with someone else. How could Jesus do this with a person like Zacchaeus?

Later on, it is likely Zacchaeus held a party for his esteemed guest as tradition would have dictated. As the host, he got up at the end of the evening to give a speech. It would be likely that most of the other guests were fellow tax collectors. Imagine their amazement as Zacchaeus said, 'Look Lord! Here and now I give half of my possessions to the poor, and if I have cheated anybody out of anything I will pay him back four times' (Lk. 19:8).

Now let me ask you a simple question. If Jesus had demanded that Zacchaeus should do this when he first met him in the crowd, what would have happened? Zacchaeus would have thought Jesus was just like the other religious leaders and would have gone away disappointed and totally unchanged. But what Jesus did was not to begin with what Zacchaeus was doing but who he was. To put it bluntly, Jesus was not starting with his deeds but his needs.

The problem with many of our churches is that when people from outside approach us, we start with what they are doing, their behaviour, and not with who they are. The danger is their first encounters with us are characterised by being told that the way they live their lives is totally wrong and they need to stop now. That doesn't tend to make people to want to stay around. But when people find their needs, such as security, acceptance and appreciation, are being met, they are attracted to the community and there is much more likelihood their actions might radically change as well.

So at the Net we spent time thinking about our needs and the needs of others within and outside the church. We used lots of materials from David Ferguson and others to help us do this.[28] The material helped us to think more about ourselves and others and how practically we could carry out Jesus' command to love our neighbours. We looked at how God had created us with needs for such things as support, encouragement, approval etc. and how we might begin to meet them for each other. In the first six months, we spent time looking at these kinds of issues as we got to know each other and we would often revisit the materials over the following years. The great thing about this teaching is that it applies to you as a human being, whether you are a Christian or not, and as people found their needs met, we discovered they wanted then to meet others' needs. This wasn't just a narcissistic exercise but a real attempt to show love to one another practically. If you join a community and suddenly your relationship with your partner or child improves dramatically, then you tend to want to find out more. This faith stuff suddenly seems very relevant.

It also helps people to see personal evangelism in a new light. If evangelism starts with being with people and learning to meet their needs, then surely we all can do that? It is part of being human. But in doing that we are enabling people to experience something of the love of God, who made us with these needs.

We started using this relationship material in our local gym with gym members who signed up for a four week course. It was amazing to see these people with no church background discovering they had been made with needs, like everyone else, and how they could meet needs and have others meet theirs.

Factor 4   A shared emotional connection

What kind of shared history is being developed?

Finally, for any community to flourish there needs to be a shared sense of history. This involves an acknowledgement of where you have come from; a retelling of victories, bruises and failures. This can easily be overlooked in church life but is vital to good community sense.

We tried to do this in two key places. One was our weekend away which was always a highlight of our year. Often people joined us for the weekends who were on the edge of our community and it was often a significant part of them moving further in. This was a place where we enjoyed being together. We tried not to have too much formal input, usually three sessions, but lots of time to be together and have fun. In this fun there was lots of shared emotional connection. Often parts of the church's history were retold or people told their own stories and the role the Net played in them. It was always a wonderful and exhilarating time.

The other forum for our emotional connection was our church birthday, celebrated on the first Sunday of October each year. Initially the Net was only given three years to prove itself and so each year was a celebration that we were still going and growing. As time went on, it was an opportunity to look back and give thanks and also to look forward to the future God had for us. It also enabled new people to discover and share in the history of what had been happening with the Net. It was a time of great fun and always followed by eating together.

These four factors of membership, influence, integration and shared connections enable people to feel they belong and matter, not just to God but to one another. They also discover that their needs are met through their commitment to one another and this begins to percolate out into the wider community. Community, when it is working well, has such an attractive quality which begins to draw others in as they experience it. It is also worth saying that no community is perfect and it can also be a place of hurt and anger, as we discovered. (See Essential Nine on expectations.

I certainly have had much to learn about community in the last few years. I am so thankful to God that he taught me this before I got my hands on one! Community is often a difficult concept to describe but we know it when we meet it. This was true for one woman who began to become part of our community four years ago. She was brought to church by another woman. Initially, she was very quiet at our meetings. She had two young children who were a challenge for her to look after and it was obvious that she had a troubled past. It would have been easy to have told her to sort herself out quickly. But fortunately this didn't happen. One of our leaders simply befriended and spent time with her and her children. It was wonderful to see this fantastic leader effectively mother her. It took time and patience to begin to see real change but having experienced real love from this leader it was always likely. It was amazing when she decided to become a follower of Jesus and she stood up in front of our community to tell everybody. It was a humbling moment.

Then we discovered that she was being hounded by a loan shark. She had not taken out a large loan but, with crippling interest rates, the debt was mounting despite her repayments. We talked about this as a Leadership

Team and decided that the church should pay off the debts. We contacted the company and paid off all the money. The letter we received from her was incredible, as she thanked us for all we had done. But it left me thinking, this is exactly what church should be doing, paying off the debts of people. What a wonderful picture of the gospel this is; the paying of a debt so we could start again, free from the fears of the past. There is nothing better than community, when we do what we are meant to do.

For me, this has been some journey. I began by seeing community as something that was totally unconnected to evangelism and mission. Now I realise that these things are completely interrelated. The telling of the gospel creates community but community is also one of the main factors in our telling of the gospel as we live out Christ's life together.

Questions for discussion and reflection

1. How do you define community?

2. What importance do you attach to community as a church? How is this experienced by the community?

3. How could you further develop your sense of community?

4. How are you putting needs before deeds in your community?

5. How attractive is your community to those outside the church?

Books

David Ferguson,   *The Great Commandment Principle*
(Wheaton: Tyndale, 1998)

Donald Miller, *Searching for God Knows What* (Nashville:
Nelson, 2004)

Joseph Myers, *Organic Community: Creating a place where
people naturally connect* (Grand Rapids: Baker, 2007)

Philip Yancey, *Church: Why Bother?* (Grand Rapids:
Zondervan, 1998)

Essential Seven

Church

The essence of what we are

For the first time in hundreds of years we have to face the question, what is church? With the starting of new churches, fundamental questions are being asked about what makes a community a church or not a church. What is the minimum requirement to be church? What are the essential elements that need to be in place for church to exist? When do we stop being a group and become church?

Last week I talked to a friend, Sue, who is starting something in a local school for the parents of the children. They meet on a Thursday morning and there is plenty of coffee and food but they also watch a DVD, discuss it, talk together about their lives and pray. The majority of people who have started attending have no church background. This group isn't seeing itself as a stepping stone into 'proper church', which would operate on a Sunday in a church building, and the people who attend wouldn't think about going elsewhere to church. So are they church already or are they on the way to becoming church? How will they know and does it really matter? I think these issues are really important and need to be carefully thought through. This chapter may seem theoretical but in reality it is intensely practical in helping to answer the vital question which Sue asked me: 'Have I created a church?'

For many years we have not had to do this. Church has been like a merry-go-round. You jump on it as it continues going round and round, as it has done for ever. Either you hang on or it throws you off. But it doesn't gives you time to think about what you are actually doing. Church is simply something we go to or something we are part of. The packaging of church may differ slightly but essentially we have viewed it as an unchanging institution.

Even so, we have not been clear about what we mean by this term church. Martin Luther famously thanked God that even a child of seven knows what the church is but I don't think this is our present situation. We have mostly got beyond the notion that church is the building. But it is an interesting exercise to ask people what their church is like. Usually what they do is tell you about the programme of the church, the services, groups and meetings that the church has. Is that what defines church? Is it the sum total of its activities or is there more to it?

Part of the problem is that we use the word 'church' to cover a number of different things. We use it of a building, a denomination, of a local group of Christians and of all Christians everywhere. This is reflected in the biblical usage. For example, New Testament writers use the word church to refer both to a meeting in a house and to the church of a particular area (Rom. 16:5; Acts 9:31; 1 Cor. 16:19).

In the New Testament the word that is normally translated church is *ekklesia*. This Greek word was also used to translate the Hebrew word *qahad* which is used in the Old Testament for the assembly of God's people.

(Deut. 4:10-14) This assembly of the nation of Israel was not just a meeting of the people but a meeting of the chosen people of Israel with their God. The New Testament term builds on this. The Greek word translated as church was not originally a religious word. It is made up of two words, 'out' and 'to call' and therefore literally means a 'called out' group. It tended to be a political term for a lawful assembly in a city of all those people who had the rights of citizenship. It was convened by the call of a herald. You could see the attractions for the New Testament writers. It resonated with Israel being called out as the people of God, and reminded them that the church was to be a group called out by Christ, to whom he had given the rights of citizenship through his death and resurrection. But then we need to ask the question, what are we called out for?

When you are continuing the activities of church, you very rarely have to ask fundamental questions about what church is. Often you are keeping the thing going and making some improvements on the way. But when you start something new with a blank sheet of paper it is a different story.

Starting a new church brings you immediately to the question: 'What are we creating?' What do you have to do to 'do church'? Where do you start? The danger, as I said earlier, is that we all have an implicit default model of church which we believe is *true church*. But we need to recognise these hidden drivers for our view of church and examine them in the light of both Scripture and reality. As Michael Griffiths wrote many years ago, 'A high proportion of people who "go to church" have forgotten what it is all for. Week by week they attend services in a special building and go through their particular, time-honoured routine, but give very little thought to the purpose of what they are doing.'[29]

You may wonder why I have included chapters on community and church. I think community reflects the bigger issues of the nature of God and our humanity, and church is a particular part of that. Simply speaking, not all communities of Christians are church but all churches must be communities. So what makes the difference? When do you stop being a group meeting together and become a church?

I want to reiterate how important church is. One of the most significant lessons I have learnt through the Net is that church is not a sudden afterthought of God's. It reflects a God who is by his very nature community and who designed us to need each other. Lesslie Newbigin summed this up when he wrote, 'It is surely a fact of inexhaustible significance that what our Lord left behind him was not a book, nor a creed, nor a system of thought, nor a rule of life but a visible community.'[30] 'Jesus is great and I'm afraid belonging to the church is part of the package' was the implicit message I received when I became a Christian. There was an apologetic air about church that said we know it's not very good but you have to put up with it. Today that is still a popular message within and outside the church. Jesus is great but the church isn't. I have realised now that church is great too, and I want to tell you why.

Church is essential

The descriptions of church in the Bible suggest the importance that God attaches to it. There are many images that are given for the church in the New Testament. Two of the images are stunning in what they say.

The body of Christ

This image is used by Paul (Eph.1:22–3). It is amazing that Paul says the church is Christ's body. Do we see it as that important? We are not only a body of people but the body of Jesus. Church is more than a corporation of individuals; there is an organic unity, based in our new creation in Christ.

The bride of Christ

Even more amazing is the image of the church as the bride of Christ. It describes an intimate union of Jesus and his people which will be consummated in heaven. This image has its roots in the Old Testament (Is. 54:5–6, 62:4-5). It highlights the special nature of the church, its preciousness to Jesus (Eph. 5:25–33; 2 Cor. 11:2) and the importance of our response to the groom. 'Our call is to first to be the bride faithful but that is not the total call. The call is not only to be the bride faithful, but also the bride in love.'[31]

So having looked at what the Bible says about church, what is the basic DNA of church? What are the essentials that make it church, whatever the culture and time? This is a question we have not faced for a very long time but there have been various attempts throughout history, starting from the Donatist controversies of the fourth century AD, to state the marks or notes of the church. I have found a particularly helpful model in thinking about the marks of the church in the Mission Shaped Church report.[32] Four particular marks of what it means to be church are identified, developing on the work of Mike Breen.[33]

1. The Upward Dimension

Primarily a church needs to enable people to develop their relationship to God. It is more than a group of people who get along well with each other. A church must be a place where people encounter God, both corporately and individually. This is all about worship; not only in the sense of a weekly service but of lives that are giving God his worth in all aspects of life including work, home and social life.

The Archbishop of Canterbury, Rowan Williams, suggests that, 'Church is the event of Jesus' presence with its characteristic event of gathering people around him . . . The church is what happens when Jesus is there, there received and recognised.'[34] It has at its core this upward dimension and stresses that this meeting with Jesus and experiencing his new life is not a one-off phenomenon. We need to think about what we do as church to help nourish that upward relationship. Williams challenges us in his sermon to think about this, when he asks

> Are there structures and patterns which let that basic event of encounter happen again and again? Because if not, the church has become something very different from where it started; it has become a community which says once there was an encounter with Jesus and we like to remember that . . . We have to ask much more radically, how do we structure a society in which it goes on being possible, even likely, that people will meet Jesus and, in meeting Jesus, will want more people to meet Jesus?[35]

What a great challenge! It is so easy to become a community that can only relate to what happened in the past with Jesus but has no story of the present. How do we ensure that this upward dimension ensures a continuing encounter with Jesus? It is a demanding question to ask of our worship activities.

At the Net, we tried to inculcate an expectation that people would meet Jesus through our worship. This meant thinking about how and where this might happen and to allow space for that encounter to happen. We tried to enable people to use all their senses in worship, not just their ears and eyes. We learnt lots from the alternative worship people about this: creating opportunities for people to touch things or enjoy evocative smells. We also tried to give people a choice. One of the dangers of church is that someone at the front tells you how to respond but the problem is it may not be a way that suits or helps you. So we would often have spaces where people could respond, especially after the talk. There would be something to see on the screen for those who wanted to stay seated. But there might also be an opportunity to light a candle and pray, to write a message to God and attach it to a wooden cross, or to be anointed with oil.

We rediscovered the power of the church's sacraments of communion and baptism to help us encounter Jesus. I had come from a tradition where often the communion service was tacked on the end of the service and was something we had to get through quickly but I soon found that communion was a very powerful symbol of that encounter with Jesus as we receive the bread and wine. It was often at this time that people felt able to experience his presence. We had all ages present for the communion and encouraged anybody who was a disciple of Jesus, whatever their age, to partake of the bread and wine. It was often a most profound moment. It is worth noting that John Wesley, the founder of Methodism, believed that communion could be an evangelistic medium that drew people into the church, describing it as 'a converting ordinance that proclaimed the cross'. (See 1 Corinthians 11:26, from which Wesley argued communion was an act of proclamation.)

We also found baptism was an important event for people to encounter Jesus and to mark their encounter with him. In one of our services, we inflated a large paddling pool to create a makeshift baptismal pool. It was wonderful to see people of all ages being baptised and affirming their faith in Jesus. The only problem was that the hot water tank we were using was very small and so it was a real breathtaking experience for those going under the water!

We had to challenge people's default position. For a number of people who helped me start the church, worship was simply singing modern worship songs. But is this really all worship is? So at a number of our services we didn't have any worship songs or even a band playing music! Some people thought I was crazy but we soon discovered that there were lots of other ways to worship God. We also stressed that we could worship God when we weren't gathered together as church, as well as when we were.

2. *Inward dimension*

Although the upward dimension is primary there is more to church than 'my relationship with God'. As we have seen in the previous chapter, it is also about meeting God with each other. To repeat Rowan Williams' comments, 'Church is the event of Jesus' presence with its characteristic effect of gathering people around him and making them see one another differently as they see him.'[35] The transforming work of the cross is not limited only to our relationship to God; it extends to our relationships with each other. What unites us is our relationship to Jesus but we are also being changed in how we see each other. There is the opportunity to come together and, as Paul says, to destroy the barriers that come between us (Eph. 2:1–22).

3. Outward Dimension

The third dimension is the priority of those who are outside the church. This has been discussed in Essential Five. The church cannot only be about our relationship to God and ourselves, it must connect with the world outside the church. 'The church is the only society that exists for the benefit of its non members,' as William Temple, a former Archbishop of Canterbury, is famously quoted as saying.

4. Belonging Dimension

Often books will talk about dimensions of up, in and out but the Mission Shaped Church Report added a fourth dimension. It emphasises that any one church is not fully church if it sees itself in isolation from the rest of God's people or from the history of God's church. To belong is to recognise that your church is a part of something much bigger in the present, past and future.

The present
We belong in **the present** to a worldwide, national and local church.

At the Net, I emphasised that we were part of the churches in Huddersfield, the Church of England, part of the church in England and part of a worldwide church. We would invite people from other churches to speak and would have visits from our local bishop. We supported one of our church members who worked in developing Christian radio for local radio stations. We supported some missionaries working in the Muslim community in Bradford. We also linked up with a church in Taiwan who had similar aims to us. Their leaders came over to visit us and we sent a team over to work with the church in Taiwan for ten days. For some of our people who had recently come to faith, it was the most amazing experience to see God at work in a different culture and continent. I also encouraged people to go to national conferences and conventions again to understand how they were part of something much bigger.

We also tried hard to work with other local churches, especially in sharing our resources. For example our youth leader and some of our young people helped another church to run a holiday club in a tough area of Huddersfield. Two of our church helped Wakefield Cathedral with an audio project they were developing.

This belonging also meant we were accountable to other people for what we were doing. There is no place for being a 'stand alone' church. I was ultimately accountable to the Bishop of Wakefield but the church also had an Advisory Group which helped us plot our way forward.

The past
We share in **the past** story of the church.

This is highlighted by passages like Hebrews 12 where the writer reminds us of the cloud of witnesses of the past who surround us as we journey forward. We are foolish if we believe that the issues we face today are original to us. Many of the things we grapple with now have been confronted before. We need to see ourselves as part of the church's history, learning from those who have gone before us.

The future
We anticipate **the future** of the church in eternity.

In the future we will be part of the eternal church that is gathered together to be with God (Rev. 21). What we are now together as church is only a small part of what we will be when God comes to his church.

You may be thinking this all sounds very theoretical and dry. But to create something new we need to know what we are forming. How can you tell whether your group is really church and that it has the potential to sustain itself for the long term?

These four dimensions give you a good starting point for the DNA of church but it is only a framework upon which you then start to develop something for your context. The four dimensions don't tell you whether to have a building, what type of music to have, if you should have a small group system or how to do your evangelism. The next step is to develop the characteristics of church in your particular context.

There is not going to be a simple blueprint to follow. I see many new churches beginning which are really only clones of the church the starting team have left or a pale imitation of 'successful' churches they have visited. The whole way they do their worship, community and mission is simply a copy of what they have experienced before. But the danger of this is that a whole set of local circumstances and factors are ignored. We don't need more cloned churches: we need new churches which are willing to do the hard work of asking creatively what worship, community, mission and belonging might look like for their particular area. This doesn't mean we can't learn from others but then we have to take the lessons we have learnt and apply them in our own situation. Church

will look different on an inner city estate, in a pub, for
business people, for goths and so on. But underneath its
particular manifestation, any church will share a DNA
that makes church, *church.*

I think that it is important that we continually review
whether what has been developed is true to both the
DNA and the local context. Are you really creating
church for a particular location or have you lapsed into a
default position which does not reflect your vision or
your context? Church leaders should reflect periodically
on what is happening and maybe make some changes
and some further developments. It is very helpful when
doing so to have help from people outside the church
who are positive supporters but who can also give you
good criticism of what you are doing.

At the Net, I had great support from our Advisory
Group. They met with me three or four times a year to
talk through issues concerning the church. We took some
time to conduct a review after two years, to see if the
ideal was becoming a reality in our situation. We worked
on a number of questions which were

- Is it authentic church? Is it exhibiting all four
  dimensions?
- Is it Anglican and what does this mean when you are
  not using the traditional language and ceremonies?
- Using a mission health check, we asked, Is it healthy?
- Is it sustainable? Does it have a long term future in
  terms of leadership, finance and growth?
- Is it fulfilling its original calling? Particularly, is it still a
  church trying to work through networks of relationships and is it connecting with unchurched people?

The development of the questions and our answers to
them helped the Diocese to decide if we should continue

with their backing but they also helped us to see how we were developing as a church and if we were being true to our calling to be a people called out to enable others to follow Jesus.

As well as thinking what church is and how that might work out in a particular context it is also worth thinking out how churches generally have been developing over the last fifty years. As churches respond to their culture there are bound to be changes to how we do some aspects of church. It can be very confusing today reading about church with all its varying titles and categories, with terms such as 'traditional church', 'emerging church', 'new forms of church', 'seeker church', 'fresh expressions of church' or 'purpose driven church'. It is helpful to think about how things have changed and developed and maybe where your church fits in and what you can learn from others. See Appendix 1 for some categories I have found useful.

The development of new churches is making us focus again on the fundamental issue of what the church is and hopefully away from believing that the church is a necessary evil. Again and again with the Net, I had to ask the question 'Why we are doing this?' and 'How does it enable us to be truly church in the networks of Huddersfield?' The longer I was involved with the Net, the more committed I became to this amazing community that we call church. We all know that churches are far from perfect but church is God's Plan A for his world and there is no Plan B. Church is the community of God's people, with all their strengths and weaknesses, on mission together.

Questions for discussion and reflection

1. Do you see church as blessing or pain?

2. Do you see your church as 1.1, 1.2 or 1.3 (see Appendix 1)?

3. How would you try to define the marks of a church?

4. Using the four dimensions, which dimension is strongest for your church and which weakest?

5. What is being done to encourage your church to see that it is part of something bigger?

Books

Steven Croft (ed), *The Future of the Parish System* (London: Church House, 2006)

Steven Croft, *Transforming Communities* (London: DLT, 2002)

Bill and Lynne Hybels, *Rediscovering Church* (Grand Rapids: Zondervan, 1995)

A.E. McGrath, *Christian Theology: An Introduction* (Oxford: Blackwell, 1993). See Chapter 15 on the church, an excellent theological and historical background.

Essential Eight

Discipleship

Growing more like Jesus

Jesus' commission is to make disciples, not converts (Mt. 28:18–20). The danger for new churches is that our energies flow into getting people into church and we think at this point our work finishes. But this is only the start of their journey with Christ and our role as a church. Paul reminds us of our whole purpose when he writes, 'We proclaim him, admonishing and teaching everyone with all wisdom, so that we may present everyone perfect in Christ' (Col. 1:28). The word translated 'perfect' here can also be translated 'mature'. It must be our task to see people grow, develop and mature in their relationship with Jesus. That is a long term task we are committed to. John Stott, in one of his last public speaking engagements, said that, 'Christlikeness is the will of God for the people of God.'[36] It also requires everyone to recognise we are all disciples, however long we have been Christians. This is not something for a season or for new believers, but is the work of our lives with the help of the Holy Spirit.

My aim here is not to lay out a discipleship scheme for your church; I think the issue is more complex than that.

More importantly, I do want to affirm the importance of this Essential for the long term health of your church. It will not just happen but needs to be considered and planned for.

In our present climate of falling church attendances and a diminishing knowledge of the Christian faith, this requirement for discipleship is even more important. Unchurched people often now come with little or no background knowledge of Jesus or the ability to live out a relationship with him in everyday life. They need help to see how this new relationship with Christ and his people will impact every area of their being and their lives.

We also need to make sure that our evangelism does not have a soft sell approach to the gospel. It is possible to give the impression that Jesus is there to meet our every need and to give us health, wealth and happiness, while simply asking for our assent to some doctrine. Someone who became a Christian at the Net said, when her life developed some serious problems, 'But Dave, I didn't sign up for this.' Yet if you look at Jesus' ministry, at times he tried to make it hard for the crowds to follow him. He didn't attract them with promises of the easy life. He was never shy of making plain the cost of following him (Lk. 14:25–35; Mk. 8:34–38).

It will not just happen

One of our big mistakes in helping people to grow to maturity as disciples of Jesus is that we think this all happens by osmosis. As long as they are around church, we think they will be growing and developing. But just putting me in a gym environment will not make me fit! I need to be taught how to use the machines and given a training regime to follow. A number of writers on this subject have spelt out the differences between training and trying. Trying is about wanting to do something but with no plan to achieve it: training is about developing a plan to ensure the meeting of a goal.

Two years ago, I ran the London marathon. I could not simply decide the day before the marathon I was going to run it. I needed six months of training to develop my body to the point where I could conquer twenty-six miles. I had to start off running a few miles non stop and gradually increase the distance over time. Dallas Willard sums this up when he writes, 'to train means to arrange my life around activities I can do that will enable me, over time, to do what I cannot do by direct effort alone.'[37] Discipleship is partly about training, which is why it is related to the word 'discipline'. It asks of us all what we will do to enable this maturity to take place over time.

Discipleship is also about change. It does not and cannot happen all at once. It is a process by which we become more like Jesus. The New Testament uses the language of transformation and renewal (Col. 3:10; Eph. 4:23; Rom. 12:2). We cannot become disciples of Jesus and remain the same as we are.

As churches, we need to create the right environment for discipleship to flourish. How individually and together are we going to ensure that we will grow? It is easy to answer the question; do you want to grow in your faith? I would assume we all do. But the next question 'How do you intend to do this in the coming year?' is much more challenging.

At the Net, we became aware that we were putting most of our resources into evangelism. This was great as people were becoming followers of Jesus but we were not doing much for them beyond that. So, when we reorganised our small group system, we introduced a group for those who were new to the faith. This lasted for at least one year but people could decide how long they were part of this group. The group went over many of the basics of Christian faith, from how to pray and read the Bible to looking at spiritual gifts or the social implications of the gospel. One of the great things about the group was attendees were being disciples together, so they could support and encourage each other.

Before we go any further it is also important to say this is a spiritual activity which we do not ultimately control, unlike other forms of training. Discipleship involves our co-operation in the training process but it is God's work in us. Our role is to put ourselves in the best places to connect with the living God and then to recognise it is up to him. He may not always work in the ways we expect him to but that is up to him.

It's not good to do this on your own

Any discipline is easier to do with others. When I was training for the marathon, if I was on a long run, I would ask Heather to run with me for the last hour. The last hour of a long three hour run was always horrendous. It was so great to have her running with me at the hardest moments when my legs were aching and all I wanted to do was to quit. In our daily lives, we all need people to run alongside us.

Small groups work well in supporting discipleship but sometimes we found smaller groups of twos were even better in encouraging growth. We encouraged mentoring where an older Christian would help and support a newer disciple, or two people at similar levels in their faith could work with each other. We produced materials to help with this process. These provided ground rules for the mentoring relationship and offered some general ideas on how to proceed. Mentoring relationships do not have to be forever but can be very successful in short bursts. We did not want to be too prescriptive in our guidelines, as mentoring is more about people sharing their lives together than following some scripted worksheet.

These relationships did not always work; sometimes the two people found they could not work well together. Chemistry is important in these relationships. But I do think these one-on-one relationships can be very beneficial in developing discipleship. It can be wonderful in providing that supporter who runs alongside you.

It's intentional and accidental

I think the training analogy is very helpful but it has limits. You cannot totally plan discipleship as a curriculum or programme. It is more than transference of knowledge, it is about living out the life of Jesus in my life, in every second, minute and hour. Discipleship is more than planned meetings: it is also about seeing God in the messy parts of our day. We need to enable people to reflect on their everyday lives, to see what God is saying in those unplanned moments. Socrates is reputed to have said 'The unexamined life is not worth living.' I think this is particularly true in our busy and active lives where there is little time to stop and ponder.

This is a discipline that I have had to work on, as someone who is not naturally reflective. Some people find writing a journal to be a particularly important way of reflecting on each day. I have always struggled with this but try to set aside time each day to reflect on what God might be saying to me. It is recognising that the whole of life is a classroom, not simply the training moments. School is in all the time. What is Jesus teaching us now?

Discipleship is 24/7

At the Net, I wanted to create an expectation that people would meet Jesus not only in our corporate experiences but in the rest of their lives as well. The time we were together was very limited; maybe two hours on a Sunday and two hours in a midweek group. That's four hours out of one hundred and sixty eight. Was that the limits of our worship and the possibility of our encountering God?

One of the dangers for leaders is that, unwittingly, they create a dependency culture. So people come to church to be fed and then return the next week for another top-up of their spiritual nourishment and woe betide the leaders if they don't make it available. They can easily become 'spiritual chaplains' who offer the resources demanded of them. This is really an extension of our consumer culture. Church is another provider of a product; a spiritual one. This can be difficult when people are very insistent about what they want and what will happen if they don't get it. I believe strongly we are to offer good teaching but part of the reason for this is to enable people to supply their own nourishment for the majority of their lives when the church is dispersed. Part of my work in preaching each week was to enable people to understand how to handle God's word in the rest of their lives.

Surely to be a disciple of Jesus is a 24/7 position without downtime? This means challenging the sacred/ secular divide that scars so much of church life. This divide contends that there are parts of our lives that are more important to God, i.e. the spiritual bits revolving around church and our own prayer life, and the rest are almost God-free. But our spiritual life is not limited to what we do in church, our small group or our own personal devotions. Everything we do is part of our spiritual life, as it relates to God and how we live for him. It is wrong to limit God to church-type activities. There is no part of our lives that God is not interested in. We need to be asking how we enable people to encounter Jesus at work, in their home, their car, watching TV, eating their tea, shopping or playing sport. We also need to help them see how what is happening in our communities, our countries and our world is part of their spiritual lives. At the Net we found the Willow Creek course 'An Ordinary Day with Jesus' really useful in helping people to think through some of these issues.[38] This six week course helps people to imagine what it would be like to live one whole day with Jesus actually by their side. It takes them from waking up to going to bed at night and helps them to develop spiritual disciplines throughout their day, giving them chances to encounter Jesus. Out of this course, which we have run a number of times, a small group developed to continue working on how Jesus is present in every part of our lives, with no exclusion zones. It is vital that we are living as disciples of Jesus every day and not just when we are together as church.

It is about who we are, as well as what we do

This is not simply about how we do certain things as followers of Jesus, more importantly it is about character. This is the real me, not the public me that I show to people but the person I really am inside. It is important that we continue to take on more of the character of Jesus as well as his behaviour and actions. The fruits of the

Spirit are a great place to reflect more on what is happening inside us as we consider Jesus' character (Gal. 5:22).

It doesn't only happen in the classroom

I have usually found that people's faith grows quickest when they have to exercise it. When people from the Net visited Taiwan, helped out with the football course, ran a holiday club or went off on mission teams, those were often the times when they really developed. It was important that we regularly gave people opportunities to exercise faith beyond their normal experience. There is something about being dependent on God and doing this with others that moves us on spiritually.

Jesus' call to us is to follow him in everything we are and all we do. We needed to be continually asking as a church how we were encouraging and enabling this to happen. This is why one of our values at the Net was developing discipleship. We needed to be taking our role in presenting people mature in Christ seriously. It is important our world sees the power of changed lives. The making of disciples whose lives are changing is an incredibly powerful and attractive proposition. It is often the best way to make further new disciples.

Questions for discussion and reflection

1. How important is discipleship for your church?

2. How are you helping people to develop in their relationship with Jesus?

3. How are you encouraging people to see discipleship as a 24/7 activity?

4. What kinds of resources are you providing for people?

Books

Andy Freeman and Pete Greig, *Punk Monk* (Ventura: Regal, 2007)

L. Graybeal, and J. Roller, *Learning from Jesus: A Spiritual Formation Guide* (San Francisco: HarperCollins, 2006)

Peter Maiden, *Discipleship* (Milton Keynes: Authentic Media, 2007)

John Ortberg, *The Life You've Always Wanted* (Grand Rapids: Zondervan, 2004)

Eugene Peterson, *Christ Plays in Ten Thousand Places* (London: Hodder and Stoughton, 2005)

Paul Stanley and Robert Clinton, *Connecting: The Mentoring Relationships You Need to Succeed* (Colorado Springs: Navpress 1992)

Dallas Willard, *The Great Omission: Reclaiming Jesus' essential teaching on discipleship* (Oxford: Monarch, 2006)

Essential Nine

Pace

Being prepared for the long haul

The training for a hundred metres sprinter and a marathon runner are very different. The danger in creating church is that we are training for a sprint but running a marathon. All the energy is put into the start but little is left over for the long haul. We need to be creating churches that run at a sustainable speed for the long term and don't implode after a few years.

Part of the problem is that the pace of life generally is getting quicker. An international study commissioned by the British Council found that city dwellers are walking 10 per cent faster than they did ten years ago. Psychologists believe that walking speed provides a reliable measure of the pace of life. Professor Richard Wiseman, who led the study, commented, 'The key conclusion is that the world is speeding up. Pace around the world is 10 per cent faster than ever before. That's not great for our health. As people speed up in their lives they are not eating properly, exercising or seeing friends and family. All these things can lead to all kinds of things, especially heart attacks.'[39]

The pace of the church

Can a church have a heart attack? It can certainly lose heart in a hectic schedule and it is important to think about the pace not only of individuals but also of the church, which has, I believe, certainly increased by at least 10 per cent in the last ten years. There are so many activities and programmes to be run and all these activities need extra meetings to organise them. We then discover busy people having to take on even more responsibility at church. That's sustainable if you are a big church with a large staff team but most of us are not in that situation.

I often hear churches talking about what new things they are going to start but have rarely heard discussions about what they are going to stop doing, to free up time for these new things. We just add to the programmes and quicken the pace. The danger is that this ever quickening pace sucks the life out of us and we discover that our spiritual reserves are running on empty.

The rhythm of life

God has given us a rhythm to live by. It is inbuilt in creation. 'By the seventh day God had finished the work he had been doing; so on the seventh day he rested from all work. And God blessed the seventh day and made it holy, because on it he rested from all the work of creating that he has done' (Gen. 2:3). This principle was then enshrined in the Ten Commandments (Ex. 20:8). Now why did God rest? Was he exhausted and in need of a break? It's unlikely: probably it was to introduce this principle of rest and rhythm into his creation. In the Old Testament, other rhythms became part of the life of the people of Israel. This involved the festivals which gave them rest and space to reorder their priorities in the midst of their hard agrarian lives.

I think we need to consider a Sabbath principle of rest for the church. Initially at the Net, we went off at a sprinter's space. We were organising large scale evangelistic events monthly which took lots of planning and hard work. There were all sorts of meetings to plan activities like small groups, children and youth work; groups to think about our future strategy, developing our values; as well as planning the regular services. We were committed to excellence and so we wanted everything to be the best it could possibly be. But within a year, we realised that we could not sustain this pace if we were to survive long term. We were on the way to burnout if we did not do something.

A basic rhythm

So we started to create a pattern for the life of the church. Some of it was planned and some of it evolved. We wanted to ensure we had the ability to run the marathon, not just survive the sprint.

We stopped everything in August to enable people to have as much rest as possible. The only regular event was a weekly Sunday get-together, often in workshop form. Mainly we had people from outside the church leading this but sometimes church people talked about their work, ministry or interests. The children and youth could join in or there was often some sport activity outside or a DVD. A bring and share breakfast was often part of the time. We had considered doing nothing but we were aware that, as a community, it was important to come together as a group. This arrangement meant those that were involved every Sunday, such as musicians, youth and children's leaders, had some time off from these activities. I think it is people who are involved regularly on Sundays who particularly need some kind of rhythm to church life. We encouraged all small groups to stop meeting too but we left it up to individual groups to decide for themselves.

There was also a break on Sundays four times a year (on the fifth Sunday) when we did something for all ages socially together as a church. This was a great time to have fun together and to get to know each other more but it also gave people an important break.

We had a Sabbath principle in place which meant it was guaranteed for eight or nine Sundays per year that we would not have the usual strains of all the activities and the rotas needed to facilitate them. Weeks without rotas have much to commend them! I realise that not every church can do this but every church can think about its pace and rhythm.

I think our weekend away was the other part of our rhythm of rest. Initially we went away every other year but it was so popular that it became yearly. Again, we tried to reduce to a minimum activities that had to be organised by church people. We tried to bring people in to run our under-16's work. We used an outside speaker but we made sure that we did not pack the programme with talks and seminars but created lots of space for fellowship and fun.

What to give up?

What is being taken away to ensure that the revs of the church are not just simply increasing year on year? This is part of the reason why, when we had a main activity on a

Friday or Saturday night, we didn't then add the usual Sunday morning. We tried to use the same principle when organising training events. These are really important in helping with pace as they give people a chance to gain some input to balance all they give out; but they are another meeting in the diary. So for example we would cancel small groups when the small group leaders were doing training, so as not to add another meeting for them, or we suggested the groups met without their leaders for one week.

It is also important that we help people to develop their own spiritual disciplines, individually and corporately, which gives them space for prayer and solitude as antidotes to our fast pace. This is part of the reason we used the An Ordinary Day with Jesus training material as widely as possible.

Hurry Sickness

This was a term coined in the 1950s by two cardiologists, Friedman and Rosenman. Meyer Friedman defines hurry sickness as 'above all, a continuous struggle and unremitting attempt to accomplish or achieve more and more things or participate in more and more events in less and less time, frequently in the face of opposition, real or imagined, from other persons'.[40] Not only are individuals suffering from ever more busy lifestyles but I think churches can easily suffer from this sickness as well as the individuals within it. We become slaves to ever-expanding programmes which need bigger structures to provide them.

I love a website I found recently about church being too busy. It is called madchurchdisease.com. That is a fantastic description of the predicament of many churches:

we have madchurch disease and it's making us go crazy.

The real danger is what hurry sickness does to our souls. John Ortberg says, 'For most of us, the great danger is not that we will renounce our faith. It is that we will become so distracted and rushed and preoccupied that we will settle for a mediocre version of it. We will just skim our lives instead of actually living them.'[41] The danger of busyness is that it reduces our capacity to live out the Great Commandment, for it diminishes our capacity to love God or others fully. This is not true only for the individual: it impacts churches as well. I have visited many churches where the general feeling is a sense of tiredness. They are going through the motions but it feels disconnected from God and from those outside the church.

The pace of the leaders

This applies not only to anyone who does this role in a church full or part time, as an employee, but also to anyone in a leadership role within a church. If we are honest, probably the majority of people in our churches are exhausted, so they too might find some useful information which they can apply in their everyday lives. It is vital to remember that the pace of the leader will have a big impact on the pace of the church.

Recent research in the UK suggests that three in ten Christian leaders have felt like leaving their work for a prolonged period of time. Seven out of ten feel heavily overworked and two hundred church leaders miss Sunday activities each week as a result of stress-related illnesses.[42] Statistics also suggest that younger leaders are more likely to suffer from these symptoms. In most tests, church leaders report both high levels of job satisfaction and stress. I don't think this is a statistical anomaly: it is because leaders enjoy and are committed to their work that they can so easily overwork, which long term produces burnout. I was talking to a pioneering leader last week who realised he had been overdoing things and needed to cut back on his commitments.

Christina Maslach is one of the leaders in the study of burnout which she defines as, 'a syndrome of emotional exhaustion, depersonalisation and reduced personal accomplishment that can occur among individuals who do people work of some kind'.[44] Her work has led to the Maslach Burnout Inventory (MBI) which measures twenty-two different categories of burnout. She states that burnout is experienced as decreasing energy, yet with a desperate attempt to maintain the same pace. Burnout manifests itself in feeling like a failure, a diminishing awareness of reward, a sense of helplessness, an inability to see ways out of a problem, cynicism and negativity.

I meet many new church leaders who exhibit some burnout symptoms. I think this is often for two reasons: getting a church off the ground is very hard work and there is a sense that the work of mission should never stop. This is the result of wanting to be a missionary church. The mission of God is unceasing but we have to take a break, or we will be no good to God in his mission.

Pacing your life

I think there are three key elements in pacing your own life whether you are a leader or not. All of these elements I have struggled with and, at times, I would have to admit that I knew the truth of them in my head but not in my experience.

Time with God

This may sound very obvious but, if we are honest, how often would we be prepared to let people know about our prayer life? The danger of all our busyness is that our own time with God gets pushed out of the way. How often do I turn to the emails before I turn to God's word? How many days have I gone without praying because of all I have to do? I was struck recently by these words of Gordon MacDonald. They certainly challenged me but also brought me back to what must be central in my life. He writes

> The forming of the soul that it might be a dwelling place for God is the primary work of the Christian leader. This is not an add-on, an option, or a third-level priority. Without this core activity, one almost guarantees that he/she will not last in leadership for a life-time or that what work is accomplished will become less and less reflective of God's honour and God's purposes.[44]

All this can become more complicated when we fall into the trap of making our relationship with God an extension of our ministry and work. So our prayers are all about the work we have to do and our Bible reading is whatever we are speaking about that week. How much time do we spend with God, because he is God? How much do we simply enjoy being in his presence? Or do we want him to bless what we are already doing?

There are many good books to help you with your time with God, that can teach spiritual disciplines to nourish your life. I think developing a pattern and rhythm for our spiritual lives is vital. It will not just happen: it needs to be planned.

In my diary, I try to put in a day a month to spend with God. I know that I cannot simply sit in silence for seven hours. I need to look at a Scripture passage, maybe listen to a talk online or a CD, and pray. I find my mind wanders immediately I start praying. Into my mind comes someone I should ring urgently, a great idea for an event or an outline for a talk. I find praying at my desk disastrous. Everything that could distract me is at my fingertips. I try to find another place to pray daily, even a different chair in the study. But for these whole days, I discovered walking and praying works well for me. In Huddersfield there was a hill nearby. I would walk up the hill and sit and enjoy the panoramic view. I had the most wonderful times with God. It often felt like all my pressures drifted away as I saw things from God's perspective and understood his greatness and majesty.

As an activist though I felt guilty about praying, which sounds crazy I know. It was so easy to think of 'the work' I could be doing. But I have come to see this is the work, because it must start with God's work in me and my acknowledgement that all I do is in response to his work.

Developing a rhythm of life

I was horrified to read in a recent report that 62 per cent of clergy took less than their holiday entitlement and only 24 per cent took their day off. I am always amazed at the way Christians seem to think abandoning the Sabbath principle is acceptable. The overwhelming majority of leaders I meet have a tendency to overwork rather than not to work hard enough.

I think it is helpful to work on a yearly, monthly and weekly personal rhythm. I am aware that your stage of life, personality type, the expectations upon you, responsibilities etc. will impact your time. I will try to give you some sense of how I worked out my pace at the Net. I didn't always live up to this but at least I did have a plan and some checks and balances.

Yearly

I always put my holidays and days off in my diary before anything else went in it. I ensured I had all my holidays and that they were well spread throughout the year. I also put in my prayer days and prayer days with my prayer cell. You can also put things in like retreats or sabbaticals.

I also tried to think about the rhythm of the year, in terms of when life would be busy and when it would be quieter. So, if things were slow in July, that would balance the business of the Christmas period and therefore I didn't need to feel guilty about it.

Monthly

I needed to ensure I was taking my days off and keeping my prayer days free from other things. I also needed to check I was giving enough attention to the family and friends. There had to be some time for me to enjoy the things that sustain me, such as playing sport. I am amazed how often leaders talk about how they used to do certain hobbies but no longer have time. Make time! I discovered that God had created me with a love of sport and I was not really me when I didn't play any. It was part of my worship. Also, is there time in the month built in for study and reading?

I once filled in a detailed timesheet for a month to see how my time worked out. This was really useful to show me about my pace and how I used my time. I then talked with the Leadership Team about the findings.

Weekly

I tried to find a balance for each week. I keep the same day off each week to give it rhythm. (A day off means not looking at emails or answering work calls!) The day off was usually dedicated to Heather and the children. I also aimed to work as little as possible on a Saturday to spend time with the family and friends, including watching Huddersfield Town regularly with my son. I would also be checking that I was not out every evening and that there were gaps in the other days.

I found that one of the best tests of whether my pace was correct was how much I laughed. This was an important indication of my health. If I couldn't remember the last time I had a really good laugh with someone, I knew something was wrong; life had got far too serious.

Maintain relationships with significant others

Remember, it is not good to be alone. Busyness can so easily isolate us from other people. We need other people around us who can help us maintain a healthy pace. Family and close friends are so important in this area. They are often the first to spot that the pace has gone wrong and to tell us. Listen to them!

I am often concerned when people don't seem to have close friends, which is often a signal of an ill-paced life. Friends are essential to our well being but they need time. Make sure you are nurturing your relationships. For me friends are so important for getting me away from my 'official' role and for allowing me to be myself.

Secondly, develop relationships with those around you at work. This might include colleagues, your leadership team, other officials or leaders. You need to ensure these are positive relationships that support you and that these people are prepared to help you keep tabs on your pace.

You can do the same for them. The danger of these work relationships is that they become competitive and this often descends into who is working the longest hours. This is even valued as a badge of honour. Such views need to be challenged as quickly as possible. I have had colleagues and fellow clergy telling me I am not working hard enough because I am taking my day off regularly. Such views need to be challenged vigorously. They are neither sensible nor biblical.

There are specific people who can help you. At the Net I found a work mentor really helpful. Every other month I would go to see him for a morning. It was so useful to talk about what I was doing, to discuss issues and to seek help with particular problems.

I also have belonged to a prayer cell for sixteen years now. Three of us meet together four times a year to support and pray for each other. Our focus is not our work but our own lives. It is a safe place to talk about what is really going on for us. We have journeyed together through so many significant times.

Some people find a spiritual advisor or director helpful for developing their spiritual life. At the Net, the Advisory Group, who were experienced leaders from outside the church, were a wonderful resource: a safe place to take issues and problems and receive the benefits of their wisdom. They were a great sounding board for me, offering both support and constructive criticism.

I am concerned that new churches and their leaders develop an appropriate pace for their long term development. The problem can be that so much energy is needed to get things underway that this either leads to collapse from exhaustion or an unhealthy pace is maintained. As churches and leaders, we need to find an appropriate pace that will enable us to develop and grow.

We need to be discerning the rhythms that will produce healthy growth and not destroy people.

I do think attention to God, to patterns and rhythms and to others is the antidote to the dangers of madchurch disease. We need to be developing these attributes for the good of us all in the church.

Questions for discussion and reflection

1. How is the pace of your life at the moment?

2. What is the pace of your church like?

3. Who is helping you to develop an appropriate pace?

4. Do you have a discernible rhythm to your life?

5. Is your pace sustainable in the long term?

Books

Peter Brain, *Going the Distance* (Sydney: Matthias Media, 2006)

Stephen Cottrell, *Do Nothing to Change Your Life* (London: Church House, 2007)

Nick Cuthbert, *How to Survive and Thrive as a Church Leader* (Oxford: Monarch, 2007)

Gordon MacDonald, *A Resilient Life* (Carlisle: STL, 2006)?

Essential Ten

Expectations

What they are and who has them

The last Essential is aimed mostly at those who are leading new churches. If this doesn't apply to you, then you might feel like skipping this chapter. But I think it is worth reading to help you think about your expectations of leaders and to ensure your church is not burning them out.

I feel this Essential is vital because whenever I am in a room with other leaders who are creating new churches the conversation often comes round to how they are feeling. They often talk about how they are drained by creating something new and how the process can grind them down. They will also say they cannot imagine doing anything else but they certainly did not realise the toll it would take on them. I know of one leader who has recently left church ministry, as they could take no more of the strain of leading a new church. In the last two weeks, I have met a leader who is suffering from stress and another needing to take extra time off work to recuperate from exhaustion. These are not people who have lost the plot, or are not suited to this calling. It is draining physically, mentally and spiritually. It's very hard work when you are involved in something that is both tiring and yet so precious to you. I want leaders not merely to survive doing something new but to flourish in it as human beings.

If I am honest there were a number of occasions in leading the Net when I felt like I could not take any more. I wanted to run away and leave everything behind. I remember feeling completely drained and very alone as I battled with things going on within me and others. At times it felt like a rollercoaster of a ride, except that the dips and highs were all happening at the same time. I felt at those times that I had created a monster and it was devouring me, piece by piece. There were times when I didn't want to open my email or answer the phone for fear of what I might find or hear. At the worst, I thought I could not survive much longer and that I was going under.

As I commented earlier, a recent report has suggested that burnout amongst church leaders is high and that it is worse amongst younger leaders.[45] A large factor behind this seems to be the issue of expectations. We live with expectations all the time. We have expectations of others and of ourselves. You are expecting now! You have expectations of this book and presently I am meeting them or not. We have expectations about how our lives will turn out, about our work and our close relationships. I have expectations about the computer I am using to write this book. My expectation, being a technophobe, is that it will crash and I will lose all my writing. (So I have backed it up in three places!)

Nearly everything we do, have or are has associated expectations. But the tricky thing about expectations, whether they come from ourselves or others, is that we are not always aware of them. Many of them are unsaid or unconscious. This makes it particularly difficult to analyse what is going on. When expectations are not met, it can do something to us internally; but if we are not consciously aware of these expectations, we won't understand our reactions or those of others. A simple example comes from the early days of my marriage to Heather. She was often unhappy that I didn't always put out the dustbin for collection. In fact her unhappiness surprised me greatly. It wasn't that I was unwilling to do it but I couldn't see why it was always my job and why she was so bothered about it. This went on for a few weeks until I discovered what was really happening. Heather's dad had always put out the dustbin when she was growing up, and so her expectations were that I would do the same. Once the expectation had been highlighted, we could deal with it, but when it was unconscious it created conflict and unease between us. Expectations often reveal what is going on deep inside ourselves.

It's not just unconscious expectations which are a problem. Unrealistic expectations are like a trap we unwittingly set for ourselves or for others. Often things like conflict, stress and burnout have their roots in false expectations and yet we rarely talk about expectations in church circles.

We need to begin with our expectations of ourselves. The danger when we start a new church is that our own personal expectations are sky high. We may feel that we are going to be the next . . . (Insert the name of your favourite leader here.) Obviously it is not good to set low expectations but sometimes we set them at an unattainable level. This can be made worse if we have a tendency towards perfectionism. We can create a set of expectations that suggest, consciously or unconsciously, that we will create the perfect church, and that we will be the perfect leader. Our relationship with God will be buzzing all the time, everyone will love us, and we will lead hundreds of people to faith in Jesus and be the key person in the revival of Christianity in our generation.

As I started the Net, I was suddenly faced with the possibility that my cherished plans might go wrong. I realised that this idea I had about a church could go belly up and I had no Plan B. Having a plan and discussing it in the abstract was a very safe place to be a pioneer. In the planning and thinking, nothing could go wrong. But as soon as we started, this idea, which was so precious to me, was out in the open and it could be marred, lost or even destroyed. This produced lots of fear in me and I spent hours worrying about how I would cope if it all went wrong.

Eventually I had to go and find a friend, a trained counsellor, to talk about what was eating me up. Talking to her, I discovered my unconscious expectations were linked to my image of a perfect leader. Part of this mental picture was that the perfect leader had no fear. So the fact I felt any fear about what we were doing was bad and wrong. This became a vicious circle, as I worried even more that I had this fear. But, as I began to look at the Bible, I saw that fear was not incompatible with being a leader of something new and exciting. I was really helped by discovering that the Apostle Paul faced similar fears when he arrived in Corinth. He wrote later to the church, 'I came to you in weakness and fear, and with much trembling' (1 Cor. 2:3).

I began to see that fear is not the opposite of faith but that faith operates in the face of our fears. I needed to acknowledge my fears but not allow them to incapacitate me. Faith believes through these fears and trusts that God is at work.

I also had to realise that I was not the perfect leader but I was the leader God had chosen for this task with all my imperfections and hang-ups. I am always encouraged by

Paul's words, 'But he said to me, "My grace is sufficient for you, for my power is made perfect in weakness." Therefore I will boast all the more gladly about my weaknesses, so that Christ's power may rest on me. That is why, for Christ's sake, I delight in weaknesses, in insults, in hardships, in persecutions, in difficulties. For when I am weak, then I am strong' (2 Cor. 12:9–10).

We sometimes think of Paul as an unflinching, unfailing, granite-like leader. Yet here he is telling the Corinthians of his weakness and recognising that God might work through him more powerfully in that state.

Another problem with our own expectations shows up when we meet with other leaders. These can be dangerously competitive times. I could so easily find myself comparing how the Net was going with other churches. I would then either feel good about myself or very down. I had expectations about how I would do, compared to others, which were not right or helpful. I was often reminded of Jesus' words to Peter at the end of John's gospel, when Peter wants to know John's future. Jesus says to him, 'If I want him to remain alive until I return, what is that to you? You must follow me' (Jn. 21:20–23). I often felt Jesus say those words to me as I tried to compare myself to others: 'What is that to you?' Our task is to follow Jesus and to do what he asks, not to play the game of creating a league table of leadership ability in our heads.

It is important to unmask those expectations that we all have and particularly to confront unconscious and unrealistic expectations. Once we are aware of them, we can then start the process of being free of the harm they do to us.

Dr Sara Savage lists six possible expectations for church leaders:

1. I must be successful in everything I do.
2. Everyone must accept me.
3. Everyone must love me.
4. If I make a mistake I am a total failure.
5. If I disagree with someone they won't like me.
6. My value as a person depends on how other people view me.

It's not surprising she adds, 'Holding these kinds of beliefs, clergy are likely to feel swamped by people's expectations.'[46]

It's difficult enough with what's going on inside us but we then have to deal with the expectations of other people in the church. This can be even harder, as it requires both you and them to be aware of what is happening. I think at the Net I found this the most draining part of my ministry.

This whole area was a massive learning curve for me. I remember one week having a church member telling me in no uncertain terms that I should be a stronger leader. They suggested that I was too weak and needed to take the lead more often and that I shouldn't let people do what they want within the church. The problems in the church were down to my leadership style. In the very same week, a couple came to visit me to tell me, again very directly, that I was far too dominant, stifled debate and imposed my own will on what was happening in the Net. The problems in the church were down to my leadership style. I soon realised that they couldn't both be right, and that this might be saying more about their expectations of leaders and their past experiences. In dealing with expectations, I have learnt some lessons the hard way.

You cannot be universally liked all the time

For someone like me who enjoys being a people-pleaser, this was a hard lesson to accept. But I had to understand I could not personally meet everyone's expectations of me. All I could do was to follow God's call for us and be authentically me. I was called to be a leader and occasionally this meant being involved in decisions that not everyone liked.

The danger is that a kind of collusion can be established. We want to fulfil people's requirements of us, because that is how we receive approval from them, but to receive what we want from them, we have to keep everyone happy.

I think one of the biggest expectations this caused me to challenge was that we all could have the Net exactly the way we wanted it. I remember some people saying that what we were doing was too different, while others complaining that we were not radical enough. It was impossible. I think I shocked them when I told them that the way we did things was not exactly how I would choose but that was not the point of the church. This was why the vision statement and our values were so important because they gave us grounds for decisions that were beyond personal taste. Leadership is not a popularity poll: it is about enabling a community to live out its God-given life. It's also worth remembering that even Jesus was not universally liked in his earthly ministry.

Beware of the default position

As I have said earlier, the default position is often an expectation based on previous experience. We all do it. This is how I enjoy singing God's praises, so this must be the right way, even the only way. Or this is how I have always done Bible study so this is the only proper way to do it. People often feel passionate about these issues, although they may not feel sure why. The danger is that they become tests of true orthodoxy and therefore people write others off if they do not agree with them. Beware of the positions people bring into a new church set up which come from their experience of previous church. It is important to help people see that although they are good things in themselves, they may not be right for the new situation.

Be aware of expectations you may inadvertently be creating

The danger with starting something new and exciting is that everyone's expectations are sky high, including your own. To some extent, that is right. It would be strange to start something with low expectations. But as soon as you use words in talking about the church like 'new', 'exciting', and 'groundbreaking', you are creating massive expectations.

I sometimes feel this is exacerbated by our talk concerning community. We can give the impression in starting a new church that our aim is to create perfect community. We can be reacting against all our negative experiences of church. This will be the place that finally gets it all right and solves all the church's problems. We will be the place where we love authentically, where all masks will be removed, where everyone is accepted, and where all are united in complete harmony. I do think we should be moving towards these things but we cannot create perfect community.

I was greatly helped by reading Jean Vanier and Dietrich Bonhoeffer's expectations of community as I battled with this issue.[47] Vanier's experiences of community came from his work in founding and developing the L'Arche communities, for people with learning disabilities and their assistants. But he didn't have a rose-tinted view of community. He says, 'There is no ideal community. Community is made up of people with all their richness, but also with their weakness and poverty, of people who accept and forgive each other, who are vulnerable with each other. Humility and trust are more at the foundation of community than perfection.'[48]

This seems to me to be a wonderful corrective to our unrealistic expectations of creating a perfect community and a fantastic description of what the church should be becoming. The German pastor Dietrich Bonhoeffer, writing just before World War Two, warns of the dangers of our expectations

> Innumerable times a whole Christian community has broken down because it has sprung from a dream wish ... The sooner this shock of disillusionment comes to an individual and to a community the better for both ... Every human wish dream that is injected into the Christian community is a hindrance to genuine community ... He who loves his dream of community more than the Christian community itself becomes a destroyer of the latter.[49]

I am excited by all the present talk about community but we must make sure we do not give the message we are creating the perfect community. We must have expectations but they must be real, and out of those emerges true community. Vanier would argue that it is in living in imperfect community that God is able to graciously deal with us and to lead us forward. He says, 'Stop running after the perfect community. Live your life fully in your community today. Stop seeing the flaws – and thank God that there are some! Look at your own defects and know that you are forgiven and can, in your turn, forgive others and today enter into the conversion of love.'[50]

When we began the Net I think many of us, including myself, had unrealistic expectations of our newly forming community. A few people who joined us saw the Net as their last hope for church. Some had had bad previous experiences at previous churches and were on their way out of church, unless the Net could save the day. Some were also trying to work through some very deep and complex personal issues. All their hope was invested in the Net, both for themselves and the future of the church. I now realise that we could not simply deliver on this: it was impossible. I remember the speaker, Greg, saying at our first church weekend, 'Don't join this church if you expect joining the Net will deal with all your personal problems.'

Of course, those who expected so much quickly discovered that this new community was not perfect. I am sure that there was more we could have done and at times we could have shown more compassion but I realise now that we had set ourselves up for a fall with some of them. We could not start something new and create a community that solved all their problems.

In not meeting their expectations, the accusation was that we had let them down and hurt them. Somehow it was my fault and the church's fault. It was a very hard time because we desperately wanted to support them. But there were only a few of us and we could never give all that was expected. On reflection, I realise we could never have done so, because we had not understood the expectations we had created for each other.

There is, psychologists tell us, a serious condition called cognitive dissonance which severely distorts the difference between the reality and the ideal. I am not suggesting we face the intensity of this turmoil in church but it is important that we learn to call people towards the ideal but teach people also how to live with the reality. We need to help people to see discord as a constructive energy that leads us forward, rather than something destructive which produces frustration, disappointment and anger.

Try not to take it too personally

This can be hard in two ways. Firstly, the danger is that the attack on the church becomes an attack on you and your character, style, personality etc. Try to keep some distance from it if you can. There may be some substance in what is being said but this does not mean you are a useless person, leader or Christian.

Secondly, it may not be meant as a personal attack but that is how you take it. The danger is that you personalise it. So if someone tells you they are not happy at church, you think it must because you have done or not done something. You should have visited them more, or you should have welcomed them more enthusiastically last week or you should have given a better talk. But sometimes you have to recognise that their unhappiness may be totally unrelated to you. If you personalise everything, you will exhaust yourself emotionally and become a workaholic, trying to do things you feel are lacking in the church. Be particularly wary of 'should', it can be a very dangerous word. It can lead you to work madly to cover up issues within yourself or to fulfil others' agendas with no reference to what God's agenda might be.

Recognise that some of this is nothing to do with you or the church

I was greatly helped by someone saying to me that there are very few places in life where people can let off steam. For example it's often difficult to do it at work because of what the boss would think and even at home it may be too dangerous. But the church is one of those places where people still feel free to say what they think. Sometimes their difficulties with church are simply transference from their problems at home, at work, or with issues within their own beings, but the church is the place where some of the hurt can escape. So the issue they are complaining about to you may not be the *real* issue but this is often very difficult for them to see or acknowledge. I was aware of this sometimes when people's annoyance with church seemed to go way past the minor point they were raising. They seemed to be at a ten in terms of their frustration or annoyance for a problem that probably should only have ranked as a three. This was often a strong hint that there was something more going on.

They might be right

I don't want to give the impression that everyone's expectations of you are wrong. That would put you in a very dangerous position of presumption. It is important to work through what is being said to see what they and

God might be saying to you and the church. This is where the help of some kind of trusted leadership team is so important, so that you are not left to battle with this on your own. It is important that you carefully consider what is being said but that you also communicate your response and how the church might proceed with it.

Sometimes you need to end the discussion

Occasionally people would come back to me and say that as a leadership team we were not listening to them. I had to graciously answer that we had heard what they were saying but as a team we didn't agree with them. This didn't mean we had no understanding of what was being said to us. One person kept coming back to us again and again with the same issue which we could not agree with them upon. In the end we had to tell them that we were drawing a line under this discussion and they needed to move on with us.

It's not good to be alone

It is very difficult to deal with expectations solo. It is important to have people around you who can help you assess whether these expectations are realistic or not. This applies both to you as a person and as a leader. As a person, you need close friends who can help you work out whether people's expectations of you are helpful or false: good critical friends who are supportive but will not just say what you want to hear are the most precious people. They need to support you when you feel you are useless and a failure as well as pointing out occasionally that someone's expectations may be valid.

As a leader you need a team around you who can help work out what expectations may be in operation. They also need to be willing to work out which expectations are correct and which need to be rejected. It is essential that this is done with others to ensure that you have the right perspective on the complexity of expectations that are operating.

Expectations are like icebergs, the bigger parts of them are submerged. They play a significant part in the life of a church, particularly a new one with all its excitement and hopes. At their worst, they can hole the church and cause it to run aground. But they can be positive in guiding the church forward if they are properly mapped and the truth of them is discerned. This is a vital role for the leadership of the church and one that is often neglected until a large crunch is heard as the church collides with something big and powerful but hidden from view.

Vanier says, 'people enter community to be happy. They stay to make others happy.'[51] I would suggest people often enter community to have their expectations met. They then find to enter fully into community they have to be willing to let some of those cherished expectations go for the sake of others both within and outside the church. This is a humbling place to find ourselves but a necessary one for us all.

I would urge you as leaders or church members to examine closely the expectations you carry. Don't let unresolved expectations hole you personally or corporately. I believe the simple lessons of this essential will help you move forward in good health.

Questions for discussion and reflection

1. What expectations do you have about yourself if you are a leader?

2. What expectations are operating within your church? Which are helpful and which are not?

3. How do all these expectations affect your well being as a person?

4. Who do you have to help you with this both as an individual and a leader?

Books

Earl Creps, *Off-Road Disciplines* (San Francisco: Jossey-Bass, 2006)

Sara Savage and Eolene Boyd Macmillian, *The Human Face of Church: A social psychology and pastoral theology for pioneer and traditional ministry* (Norwich: Canterbury Press, 2007)

The end and beyond

Looking back and looking forward

It has been a privilege to have been involved in the Net. Writing this book has reminded me of our call from God to step out for him, to step out of the box and trust him for and in the future. Heather and I were inspired by Abraham and Sarah responding to God's call to leave their country, people and family not knowing where God would take them (Gen. 12:1). Maybe God is calling you now to do something similar, to step out of the box and to respond to his call even though it's not clear what that might mean or where that might take you.

Let me encourage you. I am so glad we did it. These last few years have left me even more committed to God's mission and more sold out on the church. I want to see more communities developing who have an increasing desire to focus on helping people way outside the church to hear about Jesus. I don't feel like I am losing energy but gaining it as time goes on.

Much of what I want to say is summed up in the advert with the door handle for the Ford S-Max. In it, a man puts the handle on what seems like the sky, water or the horizon but it becomes a door into a new scene and a new world. In this way he walks from new scene to new scene until he arrives at the car. I hope that in some way this book will act like a handle that will enable you to open the door for the gospel to a new place, community or group. I do believe God is calling us, his church, to find ways to release the good news into our neighbourhoods, communities, networks and nations.

This isn't just theory. There are so many people responding to this call. Recently I talked to someone starting a church in a local school for the parents and the kids, a man who is thinking of creating church for sportspeople and another person looking to plant something in a new housing estate.

I heard a bishop say recently that we have suffered from forty years of inversion as a church and we now need to learn how to reconnect with people and culture. This will mean taking risks to enable people to hear and experience the good news of Jesus. We need leaders and churches who are ready to do whatever is required to accomplish this. I hope you are ready to take up the challenge.

In my last ever service at the Net in July 2006 I spoke from Philippians 1:6, '. . . being confident of this, that he who began a good work in you will carry it on to completion until the day of Christ Jesus.' I was very confident for the future of the Net as ultimately it was God's work, not ours. In the same way, I have great confidence for the future of the church, despite the immediate concerns about falling attendances etc. This is God's work we are being called to and therefore it is God who will complete it through and in us. There is nothing better than the church of God doing what it is called to do. As a Net member wrote so poignantly in our farewell scrapbook, 'How wonderful to belong to a church looking outwards, risking lots for Jesus, not being afraid to move, to change, to have fun, to question things, to look for and find God at work in unexpected areas. It's been painful sometimes but alive and real.'

Appendix

I have used three categories based on those in an article by Mark Driscoll, a pastor from Seattle. I have slightly adapted these.[52] As with any categories these are very general and some churches would share characteristics of them all. The categories are not an attempt to make value judgements about certain types of churches but to understand more about how churches operate.

Church 1.0

- traditional and institutional
- tends to be modernist in its thinking
- pastor/minister leads by virtue of their role/position
- holds a privileged position in the society
- services tend to be marked by hymns, robes, organ etc.
- has a pastoral mission

Church 1.1

- tends to be modernist with a post-modern twist
- pastor/minister is a manager or chaplain who markets spiritual goods and services to customers
- struggles to hold a privileged position in society
- services are marked by 70/80s pop culture
- mission is attractional based on events that bring people into church

Church 1.2

- post-modern and pluralistic
- the pastor/minister is a local enabler of missionaries
- the church accepts that it is in exile, at the margins of society
- services are a blend of ancient and contemporary local styles
- mission is done by everyone, based on relationships and moving from church into the community

Resources

On the web

www.encountersontheedge.co.uk This is from the Sheffield Centre, the Church Army's Research Unit. Through the website you can order their *Encounters on the Edge* booklet series, which tell the stories of many fresh expressions including the Net (*No.19 Net Gains*). There are also great articles and resources on the website.

www.freshexpressions.org.uk The website of the Fresh Expressions organisation, a new initiative of the Archbishops of Canterbury and York, supported by the Methodist Council. It is full of resources, articles and a directory of fresh expressions.

www.sharetheguide.org This website is the wikipedia of fresh expressions. It is a place where you can share what you have learned with others and develop learning networks.

www.emergingchurch.info This is full of stories about new churches plus articles and ideas.

www.urbanexpression.org.uk Creative church planting in the inner city in the UK.

www.emergentvillage.org American site that aims to bring together those involved in emerging churches, full of resources and articles.

www.run.org.uk The site for Reaching the Unchurched Network with lots of resources and ideas.

www.resourcechurchplanting.com Information from Resource on training in mission and starting new churches.

www.acpi.org.uk Resources, articles and ideas from Anglican Church Planting Initiative.

Books

These are books that I have found useful but have not mentioned elsewhere in this book.

Mark Driscoll, *Confessions of a Reformissional Rev* (Grand Rapids: Zondervan, 2006)
Michael Frost, *Exiles* (Peabody: Hendricksons, 2006)
Michael Frost and Alan Hirsch, *The Shaping of Things to Come* (Peabody: Hendricksons, 2003)
Eddie Gibbs, *Leadership Next* (Leicester: IVP, 2003)
Bob Jackson, *The Road to Growth* (London: Church House, 2005)
Reggie McNeal, *The Present Future* (San Francisco: Jossey Bass, 2003)

Milfred Minatrea, *Shaped by God's Heart: The Passion and Practices of Missional Churches* (San Francisco: Jossey Bass, 2004)

Doug Pagitt, *Reimagining Spiritual Formation* (Grand Rapids: Zondervan, 2003)

Doug Pagitt and Tony Jones, *An Emergent Manifest of Hope* (Grand Rapids: Baker, 2007)

Thom Rainer, *Breakout Churches* (Grand Rapids: Zondervan, 2005)

Chris Stoddard and Nick Cuthbert, *Church on the Edge* (Milton Keynes: Authentic, 2006)

Robert Webber, *Listening to the Beliefs of the Emerging Church: Five Perspectives* (Grand Rapids: Zondervan, 2007)

Endnotes

1 R.M., Belbin, *Management Teams: Why They Succeed or Fail* (Oxford: Butterworth Heinemann, 2003)

2 Dearborn, T., *Beyond Duty: A Passion for Christ, a Heart for Mission* (London: MARC, 1998)

3 This information was obtained from a talk by Robert Warren

4 Brown, C.G., *The Death of Christian Britain* (Cambridge: Routledge, 2000)

5 Beck, U., *What is Globalisation?* (Cambridge: Polity Press, 2000), p74

6 Hay, D. and Hunt, K., *Understanding the Spirituality of People who don't go to Church* (Nottingham: Nottingham University, 2000)

7 Gallup National Survey, 2006

8 Francis, L., and Richter, P., *Gone but not Forgotten* (London: Darton, Longman and Todd, 1998)

9 *Churchgoing in the UK* – A research report from Tearfund on church attendance in the UK (Teddington: 2007)

10 Warren, R., *The Purpose-Driven Church* (Grand Rapids: Zondervan, 1996), p111–112

11 For more on theology, see Williams R., *Mission-Shaped Church* (London: Church House, 2004), chapter 5, p84–103

12 Murray, S., *Church Planting* (Carlisle: Paternoster, 1998), p31

13 Finney, J., *Emerging Evangelism* (London: Darton, Longman and Todd, 2004)

14 Donovan, V., *Christianity Discovered* (London: SCM, 2001), preface to the second edition

15 Glasson, B., *I am Somewhere Else: Gospel reflections from an emerging church* (London: Darton Longman and Todd, 2006)

16 Bosch, D., Evangelism: Theological currents and cross-currents today, *International Bulletin of Missionary Research 11 No. 3*, 1987

17 Pippert, R.M., *Out of the Saltshaker* (Leicester: IVP revised edition, 1999)

18 Gibbs, E., and R. Bolger, *Emerging Churches* (London: SPCK, 2006), pp50–51

19 We used *Lost for Words* from CPAS and *Contagious Christian* from Willow Creek but there are many excellent training courses and materials available

20 Interview by Lewine Mair, the *Daily Telegraph* golf correspondent , January 2001

21 Putnam, R..D., *Bowling Alone* (New York: Touchstone, 2000)

22 Bilezikian, G., *Community 101* (Grand Rapids: Zondervan, 1997), p37

23 Ibid

24 Ibid, p34

25 Myers, J.R., *The Search to Belong* (Grand Rapids: Zondervan, 2003)

26 Ibid, p51

27 McMillan, D.W. and Chavis, D.M., Sense of Community: A definition and theory, *Journal of Community Psychology* 14, 1986

28 More details of the material on relationships we used at the Net can be found at www.relationaltraining.co.uk

29 Griffiths, M., *Cinderella with Amnesia* (Leicester: IVP, 1975)

30 Newbigin, L., *The Household of God* (London: SCM, 1954)

31 Schaeffer, F., *The Church Before the Watching World* (Leicester: IVP, 1972), p51

32 *Mission-Shaped Church*, pp96–99

33 Breen, M. and Kallestad, W., *The Passionate Life* (Eastbourne: Kingsway, 2005)

34 Williams, R., keynote address: Mission-Shaped Conference, 2004

35 Ibid

36 Stott J., *Unshackled: Living in Outrageous Grace* Keswick Year book 2007, Ali Hull (ed), (Milton Keynes: Authentic Media, 2007) p183

37 Willard, D., *The Spirit of the Disciplines* (San Francisco: HarperCollins, 1991)

38 For more details of this course, see www.willowcreek.org.uk

39 Wiseman, R., *Quirkology: The curious science of everyday lives* (London: Macmillan, 2007)

40 Friedman, M., *Type A behaviour: Its diagnosis and treatment* (New York: Plenum, 1996)

41 Ortberg, J., *The Life You've Always Wanted* (Grand Rapids: Zondervan, 2004)

42 Quoted in James Lawrence, *Growing Leaders* (Oxford: BRF, 2004)

43 Maslach C. and Leiter M.P., *The Truth about Burnout* (San Francisco: Jossey Bass Wiley, 1997)

44 MacDonald, G., Cultivating the Soul, *Leadership journal*, Summer 2005

45 Clergy work, related psychological health, stress and burnout, in *Mental Health, Religion and Culture*, 10/1 (2007), pp 1–8

46 Savage S., *The Future of the Parish System* (London, Church House, 2006), p27

47 Bonhoeffer, D., *Life Together* (London: SCM, 1954)

48 Vanier, J., *Community and Growth* (London: DLT, 1979)

49 Bonhoeffer, *Life Together*, p15

50 Vanier, *Community and Growth*, p24

51 Ibid, p36

52 Driscoll M., Lewis, C.A., Turton, D.W and Francis, L.J. A Pastoral Perspective on the Emergent Church, *Criswell Theological Review* 3/2